The Very Worst Road

The Very Worst Road

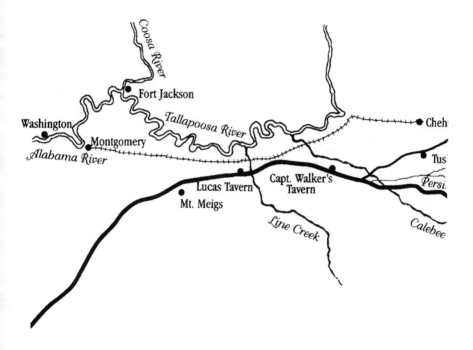

Travellers' Accounts of Crossing Alabama's Old Creek Indian Territory 1820–1847

COMPILED BY

JEFFREY C. BENTON

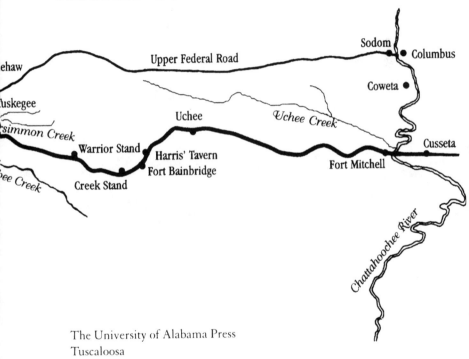

The University of Alabama Press
Tuscaloosa

The University of Alabama Press
Tuscaloosa, Alabama 35487-0380
All rights reserved
Manufactured in the United States of America

∞

The paper on which this book is printed meets the minimum require-
ments of American National Standard for Information Sciences-Perma-
nence of Paper for Printed Library Materials, ANSI Z39.48-1984.

Library of Congress Cataloging-in-Publication Data

The very worst road : travellers' accounts of crossing Alabama's Old
Creek Indian territory, 1820-1847 / compiled by Jeffrey C. Benton.
       p. cm.
   Originally published: Eufaula, AL : Historic Chattahoochee Commis-
sion of Alabama and Georgia, 1998.
   Includes bibliographical references and index.
   ISBN 978-0-8173-5550-0 (pbk. : alk. paper)
   1. Federal Road (Ala. and Ga.)—History—Sources. 2. Federal Road
(Ala. and Ga.)—Description and travel. 3. Creek Indians—Histo-
ry—19th century. 4. Alabama—History—1819-1950. 5. Alabama—
Description and travel. 6. Georgia—History—1775-1865. 7. Geor-
gia—Description and travel. I. Benton, Jeffrey C., 1945- II. Historic
Chattahoochee Commission.
   F326.V47 2009
   917.6104'5—dc22
                             2008045818

To my wife,
Karen Heydon Benton,
who loves to travel and who
has shared so many
travel experiences with me.

Contents

Illustrations

The Text

※

Several of the travel books excerpted in this volume were published in both the United States and Great Britain. Each passage is copied exactly from the original source indicated at the beginning of the chapter. Misspellings, spelling variants, and grammatical errors follow the originals. With few exceptions, errors in fact are reprinted without editorial comments.

The copies of the originals used in this volume are held by the Library of Congress or by the Special Collections, Ralph Brown Draughon Library, Auburn University. Most of the travel books have been reprinted and are easily obtainable at larger libraries.

Margaret Hall's letters were not published until 1931 after they had been edited by Una Pope-Hennessey. The excerpt from *The Aristocratic Journey* is reprinted with permission of the publishers, Penguin Putnam, Inc. of New York.

Acknowledgments

This collection of travelers' accounts would not have been possible without the meticulous attention to detail given by Cynthia Hill Townley; Madeline Rose Benton, my mother; and Karen Heydon Benton, my wife. They compared the typed text with the original books to ensure an accurate transcription.

The book and its cover were typeset and designed by Anna Jacobs Singer. Mark Stephenson drew the map that appears on the title spread.

Douglas C. Purcell's enthusiasm and the Historic Chattahoochee Commission's financial support brought the book to publication.

I also wish to thank the staffs of the Library of Congress and the Special Collections, Ralph Brown Draughton Library, Auburn University.

Foreword

From September 1994 until June 1996, I drove from Montgomery to Auburn, Alabama, several times a week. Open fields and a screen of pines border Interstate 85; the drive is easy, relaxing. After numerous trips, however, I became bored with the countryside.

As I was then researching the architectural history of Montgomery and leisure activities in antebellum Montgomery, it was not unusual that I began to wonder what the trip had been like when east Alabama was Creek Territory—before removal of the Indians in the 1830s. What I found surprised me.

I had thought that my own travel experiences had been rather varied, sometimes exciting and even dangerous. I had crossed the Atlantic on the *SS United States*, Holland's former Zuider Zee on a red-sailed fishing boat, and Japan's Inland Sea in steerage of an otherwise rather luxurious passenger ship. I had traveled by train throughout Western Europe and in the Soviet Union, India, Egypt and Mexico; by felucca on the Nile, by gondola on the canals of Venice and long-tail boat on the canals of Bangkok; and by burro-train in the mountains of New Mexico, bullock cart in India, and helicopter in El Salvador. I had raced in samlors in Thailand and pedicabs in India. I had seen the North Pole from thirty-five thousand feet, having navigated there by the stars, and had seen Cambodia's Ankor Wat by moonlight as I leaned out of an open aircraft. Crossing the Rajastani Desert in north India by open bus, my eyes, ears and nose were encrusted with sand. I was refused a room in a hotel in central Taiwan because I was so filthy after a four-hour ride in another open bus—my seat partner was a large pig in a wicker basket, and baskets of chickens fouled the racks over our heads. But none of my experiences compared to the overland travel on the old Federal Road—across the old Creek Indian territory—through what one traveler in 1831 called "the very worst road" and another in 1835, "the end of the world."

Interstate 85, which traverses east Alabama—although somewhat north of the old Federal Road—has never seemed boring for me since discovering the sixteen published accounts written by travelers who crossed from the Chattahoochee River to Line Creek from 1820 to 1847.

JEFFREY C. BENTON
Montgomery, Alabama

The Very Worst Road

1

Prologue
ᾧ

In the years before the American Civil War, travel books captivated the imaginations of Americans and Britons alike. Both
peoples were restless and desired exploration and new experiences,
even if vicariously. Two types of travel literature satisfied these
desires: that in which the travelers were required to endure hardships and overcome physical obstacles and that in which the reader
could experience a sensual escape from Victorian mores. The physical hardships of crossing Creek Indian territory—roughly from
Columbus, Georgia, to Montgomery, Alabama—fulfilled the
former requirement, and, to a slight degree, the Native Americans
fulfilled the latter.

British travelers' accounts dominate the literature. They, and
the Frenchman Auguste Levasseur and the German Duke of Saxe-
Weimar-Eisenach, came with their preconceptions, especially about
Native Americans and black slaves. In the 1820s, the Creeks, who
had been in a European-American trade system for more than a
century, were a mere shadow of themselves. Their economy was
in shambles; their men were debilitated by whiskey. Unscrupulous traders were exploiting them, and land-hungry settlers were
pressing for access to the territory of the Creek Nation. On April
4, 1832, the Upper Creeks ceded their territory by the Treaty of
Washington. In 1836 the Creeks were removed to Indian Territory
in what is today Oklahoma. The former Creek Territory west of
the Chattahoochee River was annexed to the state of Alabama.
George Featherstonhaugh includes a long, detailed account of the
trials of the Creeks, pages 102-115.

The overriding impression of the travelers' accounts presented
in this book, however, was not the plight of Native Americans and

black slaves. Rather, the physical hardships of the journey itself dominate most of the accounts.

The Federal Road linking Fort Wilkinson, near Milledgeville, Georgia, and Fort Stoddert, north of Mobile, Alabama, developed from the 1806-11 postal horse path. From a larger perspective, it was a link in the Washington to New Orleans road. For three decades the road served a variety of purposes, chiefly for settlers streaming into the Old Southwest, but also for contracted mail coaches, the army, merchants, slave traders, troupes of entertainers, and travelers.

The most hazardous segment of the road was that which crossed the seventy miles from the Chattahoochee River to Line Creek, some twenty miles east of Montgomery. This territory was the remnant of the once large Creek Nation. The situation required several military outposts, chiefly that at Fort Mitchell, just west of the Chattahoochee. The military presence was more to protect the remaining Creek territory from the encroachment of settlers, than to protect Americans traversing the territory from the Creeks.

Because of the difficulty of navigating deep sands and the more numerous waterways and swamps, the road itself was more a network of paths, rather than a single road. In 1833, a six-hundred foot covered bridge was built across the Chattahoochee connecting Columbus, Georgia, and Sodom or Girard (today's Phenix City, Alabama). Subsequently, the road was shifted northward. The Upper Federal Road traversed higher ground and was, therefore, considerably easier to navigate even in wet weather.

After the Creeks were removed to Oklahoma in 1836, there was no longer a need for a single road through the territory. The Federal Road gradually lost its usefulness as the Montgomery and West Point Railroad slowly pushed eastward from 1840. Connection was not made to West Point, Georgia, until 1851.

The best account of the Federal Road is Henry deLeon Southerland, Jr. and Jerry Elijah Brown, *The Federal Road through Georgia, the Creek Nation, and Alabama, 1806-1836*, University of Alabama Press, 1989.

2

Adam Hodgson
March 1820
۞

Adam Hodgson, a committed Christian, philanthropist, scholar, and prominent Liverpool businessman with interests in the United States, traveled nearly eight thousand miles from Maine to Louisiana, and in Upper and Lower Canada, during his sixteen-month tour that began in late 1819. Besides his commercial interests, he wanted to help repair Anglo-American relationships after the War of 1812-14.

Adam Hodgson. *Letters from North America Written During a Tour in the United States and Canada.* Vols 2. London: Hurst, Robinson and Company, 1824. Volume I, pages 121-140. In 1823, a similar account was published by the London *Christian Observer* under the title *Remarks During a Journey through North America in the Years 1819, 1820, and 1821, in a Series of Letters*, pages 145-149, 263-269. Several footnotes that are irrelevant to Hodgson's account of crossing the Creek Nation have been omitted.

We sat off as soon as it was light; and passing several creeks, arrived at the extremity of a ridge, from which we looked down into a savannah, in which is situated the Indian town of Co-se-ta, on the Chatahouchy. It appeared to consist of about 100 houses, many of them elevated on poles from two to six feet high, and built of unhewn logs, with roofs of bark, and little patches of Indian corn before the doors. The women were hard at work, digging the ground, pounding Indian corn, or carrying heavy loads of water from the river: the men were either setting out to the woods with their guns, or lying idle before the doors; and the children were amusing themselves in little groups. The whole scene reminded me strongly of some of the African towns, described by Mungo Park. In the centre of the town, we passed a large building, with a conical roof, supported by a circular wall about three feet high: close to it was a quadrangular space, enclosed by four open buildings, with rows of benches rising one above another. The whole was appropriated, we were informed, to the great council of the town, who meet, under shelter, or in the open air, according to the weather. Near the spot was a high pole, like our May-poles, with a bird at the top, round which the Indians celebrate their green-corn dance. The town or township of Co-se-ta is said to be able to muster 700 warriors, whilst the number belonging to the whole nation is not estimated at more than 3500.

About a mile from the town we came to the Chatahouchy, a beautiful river. We were ferried over by Indians, who sang in response; the Indian muses, like their eastern sisters, appearing to "love alternate song." Their dress frightened our horses; and as we were pushing from the shore, a young hunter leapt into the boat, with no other covering than his shirt and belt, and his bow and arrows slung behind. One of the boatmen had lost an ear, which he had forfeited for some infraction on the laws of his country.

We arrived at Ouchee Bridge about one o'clock; and our horses being rather tired, we determined to rest the remainder of the day at a stand kept by a young man from Philadelphia, whose partner is a half-breed. I slept in a log-cabin, without windows; and supped with my host and several unwashed artificers, and unshaven labourers, who, according to the custom of this part of the country, even when not within Indian limits, sat down with us in their shirt-sleeves, fresh from their labours. Our host had killed a panther* a few days previously, within twenty yards of the house.

*The true panther is not a native of North America, but the name is given, at least, by the common people and half-breed In-

dians, both to the Ocelot of naturalists, or Felis Pardalis, which is spotted, and to the Puma, or Felis Concolor, vel Felis Puma, which is an uniform tawny colour. In travelling in the nation of the Choctaw Indians, in the forests of the Mississippi, we started two animals, which bounded from us with a sort of careless independence. They were of a tawny colour; and as we had heard the American panther described as spotted, we concluded they were wolves, although much larger than any wolves we had ever seen. In the evening, at the log-house of our host, who was an intelligent half-breed Indian, of some consequence, we found several Indians and half-breeds; and on describing the animals we had seen, they all assured us they were panthers, which are numerous in that wild part of the country. On my observing that I thought the panther was spotted, they said some panthers were spotted, and some of an uniform yellow or tawny colour; that they often shot both.

Ouchee Creek, which is here to form the boundary between Alabama and Georgia, when the Indian title is extinguished, derives its name from the Ouchees, a conquered tribe of Indians; many of whom were long held in captivity by the victorious Creeks. We saw several of them, who exhibited in the subdued and dejected expression of their countenances, indications of their degraded condition.

Their language is a very peculiar one, and is said not to be understood by any other Indian nation. I have also heard that the children of other tribes who have been brought up among them, have been unable to learn it; but this I take the liberty to doubt. The person who keeps this house is an American, of the name of A—, from Philadelphia. His partner is Colonel L—, a half-breed, and an Indian chief. A— has a license from the United States to trade with the Indians, and is making a rapid fortune, as the charges to travellers are very high, and those who "camp out" have to replenish their corn and fodder at these distant stands, where it is sold at more than double the price which is paid for it to the Indians. Wild venison and wild turkies killed by the Indians, bacon fed in the woods, and poultry raised about the house, all cost the landlord little, whilst the absence of competition, and the necessities of the traveller, compel him to submit to any arbitrary charge. I shall give you an account of my expenses across the wilderness, when I arrive at New Orleans. The only bed-room here is a log building of one story in the yard, with three beds, such as they are; it has no window, and a clay floor, but a disposition to make the guests comfortable, which I have uniformly found, has hitherto left me nothing to regret with respect to accommodation.

So far, I have never had to admit any one into my bed-room, except my servant for one night, or I believe two. While writing, I have been interrupted and amused by Mukittaw, a fine Indian lad, half friend, half servant to my host, whom he follows on a three-year old colt, for which his master gave 70 guineas the other day in Tennessee. He has been much pleased in examining my little shaving apparatus, and my pocket inkstand; and in return, has been telling me the Indian names of different articles of dress. Here are some of them: o-kof-ti-ka, shirt; a-fat-i-ka, gaiters; de-le-shi-va-na-ta, garters; te-le-fi-ka, mocassons.

The surface of the ground continues to form a perpetual undulation. The road, which is called the Federal Road, though tolerable for horses, would with us be considered impassable for wheels.

Mobile, in the State of Alabama,
3d April, 1820

We left Ouchee Bridge on the 26th of May [March]; and early in the afternoon, arrived at Fort Bainbridge, where we found a stand in which the "Big Warrior" is a sleeping partner, and a head waiter from one of the principal inns in Washington, the efficient man. There is, however, another partner, of the name of Lewis, whom I found highly interesting. He had lived fifteen years in the heart of the Indian country, having married an Indian wife, and adopted the manners of the natives. He appeared to unite great mildness and intelligence; and has contracted so ardent a love of solitude, by living in the woods, that he lately removed his stand from the most profitable situation, because there was a neighbour or two within four miles. As he was going out to hunt in the woods, for an hour or two, at sun-set, I accompanied him, glad of the opportunity of learning some particulars of the Creek Indians, from one so long and so intimately acquainted with them. The common mode of hunting here is with a couple of hounds and a gun. The dogs soon started a grey fox, which, after running about two miles, ascended a tree. They announced that they had "treed it," as our hunter termed it, by altering their cry, when Lewis hastened to the spot and shot it. *Panthers* are *treed* and shot in a similar manner.

Lewis told me that the "Big Warrior" and the "Little Prince" are the chief speakers of the nation, or the heads of the civil department. Their dignity is not strictly hereditary, although some of the family usually succeed to it, if there be no particular objection. The chief speakers are by no means necessarily the principal *orators*, but may employ a fluent chief to convey their sentiments. Their office is to carry into effect the decisions of the great council of the nation; a deliberative body, composed of chiefs from the different towns. They assemble at Tlekotska, about fifteen miles from Ouchee Creek. They cultivate eloquence with great attention, practicing in private, or when hunting in small parties in the woods.

The most popular and influential person in the nation, is Mackintosh, the head warrior, a half-breed, under forty years of age, who is consulted on every occasion, and who, in a great measure, directs the affairs of his country. I saw him at Washington in the beginning of the year, on a deputation to the American government. His suite were at the inn where I staid; and on inquiring from one of his aides-de-camp, as I believed, (for they adopt our military terms,) if General Mackintosh had arrived, I was a little startled by his replying, "I am Mackintosh." He was very civil, and gave me an invitation to visit him, if I passed through the Creek nation, which at that time I did not contemplate.

My host regretted, in the most feeling terms, the injury which the morals of the Indians have sustained from intercourse with the whites; and especially from the introduction of whiskey, which has been their bane. He said that female licentiousness before marriage is very general, and not attended with loss of character; but that conjugal infidelity is punished by whipping, shaving the head of the culprit, and sending her naked into perpetual exile; the husband being liable to suffer the same severities, if he connive at the return of his offending wife. The murderer is now executed by public authority, the law of private retaliation becoming gradually obsolete. Stealing is punished, for the first offence, by whipping; for the second, by the loss of the ears; for the third, by death: the punishment having no relation to the amount stolen. My host remembers when there was no law against stealing; the crime itself being almost unknown; when the Indians would go a hunting, or "frolicking," for one or two days, leaving their clothes on the bushes opposite their wigwams, in a populous neighbourhood, or their silver trinkets and ornaments hanging in their open huts. Confidence and generosity were then their characteristic virtues. A desire of gain, caught from the whites, has chilled their liberality; and abused credulity, has taught them suspicion and deceit. He considers them still attached to the English, although disappointed in the little assistance which they have derived from them in late wars. This, however, they attribute rather to the distance of the British, which renders them less valuable allies than they expected, than to a treacherous violation of their promises. Whatever the first glow of British feeling may dictate, on hearing of their attachment, enlightened humanity will not repine, if, under their present circumstances, they are becoming daily more closely connected with the American government, which has evinced an active solicitude for their civilization.

Our recluse told us that they have a general idea of a Supreme Being; but no religious days, nor any religious rites, unless, as he is disposed to believe, their green-corn dance be one. Before the corn turns yellow, the inhabitants of each town or district assemble, and a certain number enter the streets of what is more properly called the town, with the war-whoop and savage yells, firing their arrows in the air, and going several times round the pole. They then take emetics, and fast two days, dancing round the pole a great part of the night. All the fires in the township are then extinguished, and the hearths cleared, and new fires kindled by rubbing two sticks. After this they parch some of the new corn, and feasting a little, disperse to their several homes. To the green-corn dance I find many Indians repair, who are settled in Alabama, on lands reserved for them by the United States, for services during the war. Many of the old chiefs are of opinion, that their ancestors intended this ceremony as a thank-offering to the Supreme Being, for the fruits of the earth, and for success in hunting or in war. The dress of the Indians is picturesque, and frequently very splendid, the scalping knife always forming a part of it, and the belts and the hems of their outer garments being often very highly ornamented. I understand that the tribes which inhabit the prairies, beyond the Mississippi, use shields. The dress of the young men under 17 or 18, is like a loose dressing gown, which they occasionally close around them; and that of the girls under 14 or 15, might be still more easily described.—The women generally are clumsy, dirty, and greasy, with long black hair, and a perpetual scowl upon their face. I saw only two handsome ones, one of whom, about 20 years of age, was very good looking. I believe when they are dressed in their gala clothes, they look much better. They are very fond of ornaments, particularly of silver. I saw one of them in her common dress selling poultry at the little inn, with four circular plates of silver hanging from her neck, the largest of which was at least two and a half inches in diameter, but very thin. I am told they have frequently fifteen or twenty. I understand that a man is allowed as many wives as he can support, and the usual number is from three to five. Mackintosh had three wives.

Lewis informed me, that the Indians often set out on long journies through the forests, without any other provision than a preparation of the flour of Indian corn, gathered while green, with honey. This mixture, dried and reduced to powder, they carry in a small bag, taking a little of it with water, once or twice in 24 hours; and it is said, that if they have the ill luck to kill no deer, or other animals, they will subsist on it for many weeks, without losing their strength: they call it *softke*.

The more reflecting of the Creeks think much, but say little of the change which is taking place in their condition. They see plainly that, with respect to their future destiny, it is a question of civilization or extinction; and a question, the decision of which cannot be long postponed. They are therefore, become very solicitous for the establishment of schools; and the introduction of the various arts, from which the whites derive their superiority. In some of these, they have already made considerable progress, many of them possessing several hundred head of cattle; and, if the warrior do[es] not literally turn his tomahawk and scalping-knife into pruning-hooks, he is satisfied to regard them as mere ornaments of dress, till hostilities shall again call him into the field; and is ambitious to attain distinction in agricultural pursuits. I saw several neat and flourishing little farms, as I passed through the nation; but my pleasure was alloyed by observing, that the labour generally devolved either on the African negro, or the Indian wife. As few of the Creeks are rich enough to purchase many negroes, almost all the drudgery is performed by the women; and it is melancholy to meet them, as we continually did, with an infant hanging on their necks, bending under a heavy burden, and leading their husband's horse, while he walked before them, erect and graceful, apparently without a care. This servitude has an unfavourable effect on the appearance of the women; those above a certain age being generally bent and clumsy, with a scowl on their wrinkled foreheads, and an expression of countenance at once vacant and dejected.

We did not leave our little cabin at Fort Bainbridge until the 28th of May [March], the 27th being Sunday. It is situated on the ridge, which separates the waters of the Chatahouchy from those of the Coosa and Tallapoosa; two wells, on opposite sides of the house, sending their streams into these different rivers. I was a little surprised to find there the son of the owner of one of the principal inns in Preston, in Lancashire, projecting the introduction of a woollen manufactory among the Creeks, under the sanction of the Natives.

Our host told me that he was living with his Indian wife among the Indians, when the celebrated Indian warrior Tecumseh,* came more than 1000 miles, from the borders of Canada, to induce the Lower Creeks to promise to take up the hatchet, in behalf of the British, against the Americans and the Upper Creeks, whenever he should require it; that he was present at the midnight convocation of the chiefs which was held on the occasion, and which terminated, after a most impressive speech from Tecumseh, with an unanimous determination to take up the hatchet whenever he should call upon them; this was at least a year before the declaration of the last war: that when war was declared, Tecumseh came again in great agitation, and induced them to muster their warriors and rush upon the American troops. It was to quell these internal and insiduous foes, that the campaign was undertaken, during which the small stockaded mounds which I have mentioned, were thrown up in the Indian country by the Americans. It was with mingled sentiments of shame and regret, that I reflected on the miseries which *we* have at different periods introduced into the very centre of America and Africa, by exciting the Indian warrior and Negro king to precipitate their nations into the horrors of war; but I endeavoured to dispel these melancholy feelings by the recollection of our Bible and Missionary Societies, and of that faithful band of veterans who, through "evil report, and good report," amidst occasional success, and accumulated disappointment, still continue the undismayed, unwearied friends, of the whole family of man.

* "This noted warrior was first made known to the public as the leader of the Indians at the battle of Tippacanoe, 7th Nov. 1811. He burst suddenly into notice, but from that time until his fall, the attention of the American people was constantly rivetted upon him. He possessed all the energy, bravery, sagacity, and fortitude, for which the most distinguished aboriginal chiefs have been celebrated, and the terror of his name alone, kept the whole line of the north-western frontier of the United States in a constant state of alarm. He was no less an orator than a soldier, and by the persuasive power of his eloquence, formed one of the most powerful confederacies which has been attempted by the Indians within the last century. He was a Shawanee." I saw his shot pouch and belt at Mr. Jefferson's, when I visited Monticello on my return to Virginia.

Soon after leaving our friends at Fort Bainbridge, we passed Caleebe and Cubahatchee swamps, and in the evening arrived at Lime [Line] Creek, which, we were told, forms at that place the present boundary line between the Creek Nation and Alabama.

We had travelled that day about 40 miles, and had passed as usual many large parties of emigrants, from South Carolina and Georgia, and many gangs of slaves. Indeed, at the edges of the creeks and on the banks of the rivers, we usually found a curious collection of sans soucis, sulkies, carts, Jersey waggons, heavy waggons, little planters, Indians, Negroes, horses, mules, and oxen; the women and little children sitting down frequently for one, two, or three, and sometimes for five or six hours, to work or play, while the men were engaged in the almost hopeless task of dragging or swimming their vehicles and baggage to the opposite side. Often a light carriage, with a sallow planter and his lady, would bring up the rear of a long cavalcade, and indicate the removal of a family of some wealth, who, allured by the rich lands of Alabama, or the sugar plantations on the Mississippi, had bidden adieu to the scenes of their youth, and undertaken a long and painful pilgrimage through the wilderness. We left Lime Creek early on the 29th, and after riding a few miles, arrived at Point Comfort; a fine cotton plantation, whose populous neighbourhood, and highly cultivated fields, reminded us that we were no longer travelling through a nation of hunters. Indeed, the appearance of oaks, in place of the pine woods, was indicative of a material change in the soil; and we soon opened on some of the beautiful prairies which you have frequently seen described, and which, as they were not large, reminded me of our meadows in the well wooded parts of England. As travellers, however, we paid dearly for the advantages offered to the landholders by the rich soil over which we were passing. Our road, which had hitherto been generally excellent for travelling on horseback, became as wretchedly bad; and we passed through three swamps, which I feared would ruin our horses. They were about a mile long each; but we estimated the fatigue of crossing any of them as equivalent to at least 15 or 20 miles of common travelling. They were overshadowed with beautiful but entangling trees, without any regular track through the verdure which covered the thick clay in which our horses frequently stuck, as much at a loss where to take the next step, as how to extricate themselves from the last. Sometimes they had to scramble out of the deep mire upon the trunk of a fallen tree, from which they could not descend without again sinking on the other side. Sometimes we were so completely entangled in the vines, that we were compelled to dismount to cut our way out of the vegetable meshes in which we seemed to be entrapped. These swamps are ten times more formidable than even the flooded creeks, over two of which, in less than three miles, we had this day to have our horses swum by Indians, whose agility in the water is beautiful. The traveller himself is either conveyed over in a boat, or, if the creek is very narrow, crosses it on a large tree, which has been so dexterously felled as to fall across and form a tolerable bridge. We slept that night at a poor cabin just erected, and setting off early on the 30th, and passing by Pine Barren Spring, and two very bad swamps, stopped to breakfast at a solitary house, where our host's talkative daughter made breakfast for us. She could not refrain the expression of her surprise at the sight of a white servant, having never seen one before, and was much more astonished when I told her, that the white and black servants in my country eat at the same table. Although of the poorest class of American emigrants, in a log-house, pervious to the weather in all directions, she said she had rather "fight a funeral than eat with a "black."

Before breakfast, we had ridden a few miles with a Mississippi Planter, of a plain, respectable cast. He had removed from South Carolina to the State of Mississippi, 15 months since; was returning home from an equestrian journey of nearly 3000 miles, commenced on the 1st January, and proposed taking East Florida in his way, in order to see if any of the rich lands there, afforded an inducement to move again, as he said he could sell his Mississippi purchase at a profit, which would amply compensate him. His estate is 70 miles from New Orleans, and he wished to be nearer his market.

We arrived in the evening at a few palings, which have dignified the place with the appellation of Fort Dale . . . .

3

Auguste Levasseur
April 1825
ॐ

AUGUSTE LEVASSEUR ACCOMPANIED THE MARQUIS DE LAFAYETTE
AND HIS SON, GEORGE WASHINGTON LAFAYETTE, ON THE GENERAL'S
1824-25 AMERICAN TOUR. DURING THE FOURTEEN-MONTH TOUR,
LEVASSEUR SERVED AS THE GENERAL'S SECRETARY, A POSITION HE CON-
TINUED TO HOLD FOR THREE YEARS AFTER THE PARTY RETURNED TO
FRANCE. FROM 1829 LEVASSEUR WAS INDEPENDENTLY EMPLOYED, AND
ONLY THEN FELT FREE TO PUBLISH THE ACCOUNT OF THE AMERICAN TOUR.

Auguste Levasseur. *Lafayette in America in 1824 and 1825;
or Journal of a Voyage to the United States.* Volume II, 171-
87, 1829. Translated by John D. Godman. Reprint edition,
New York: Research Reprints, 1970. Volume II, pages 75-83.

It was on the banks of the Chatahouche that we met with the first
assemblage of Indians, in honour of the general [Lafayette]. A great
number of women and children were to be seen in the woods on
the opposite bank, who uttered cries of joy on perceiving us. The
warriors descended the side of a hill at a little distance, and hastened to that part of the shore at which we were to disembark. The
variety and singular richness of their costumes presented a most
picturesque appearance. Mr. George Lafayette, who was the first
that landed, was immediately surrounded by men, women, and
children, who danced and leaped around him, touched his hands
and clothes with an air of surprise and astonishment, that caused

him almost as much embarrassment as pleasure. All at once, as if
they wished to give their joy a grave and more solemn expression,
they retired, and the men ranged themselves in front. He who appeared to be the chief of the tribe, gave, by an acute and prolonged
cry, the signal for a kind of salute, which was repeated by the whole
troop, which again advanced towards the shore. At the moment
the general prepared to step on shore, some of the most athletic
seized the small carriage we had with us, and insisted that the general should seat himself in it, not willing, as they observed, that
their father should step on the wet ground. The general was thus
carried in a kind of palanquin a certain distance from the shore,
when the Indian whom I have spoken of as the chief, approached
him and said in English, that all his brothers were happy in being
visited by one who, in his affection for the inhabitants of America,
had never made a distinction of blood or colour; that he was the
honoured father of all the races of men dwelling on that continent.
After the chief had finished his speech, the other Indians all advanced and placed their right arm on that of the general, in token
of friendship. They would not permit him to leave the carriage,
but dragging it along, they slowly ascended the hill they had previously left, and on which one of their largest villages was situated.

During our progress I drew near to the Indian chief; I supposed that as he spoke English, that he, like Hamley, had been
educated in the United States, and this I found to be the case. He
was about 28 years of age, of a middle height; but the symmetry of
his limbs was perfect, his physiognomy noble, his expression
mournful; when he was not speaking he fixed his large black eyes,
shaded by a heavy brow, steadfastly on the ground. When he told
me that he was the eldest son of M'Intosh, I could not recall, without emotions of sorrow, the imprecations I had heard poured forth
against this chief, on the preceding evening. [The Creeks had executed Chief William McIntosh a short time before Lafayette's
visit because he had violated a Creek agreement not to sell more
land to the whites; Chillie, the chief's son, also signed the treaty
with the whites and barely escaped execution himself.] This, in all
probability, occasioned the air of depression and thoughtfulness I

remarked in the young man; but what I afterwards learned in conversation with him explained it still more satisfactorily; his mind had been cultivated at the expense of his happiness. He appreciated the real situation of his nation, he saw it gradually becoming weaker, and foresaw its speedy destruction; he felt how much it was inferior to those which surrounded it, and was perfectly aware that it was impossible to overcome the wandering mode of life of his people. Their vicinity to civilization had been of no service to them; on the contrary, it had only been the means of introducing vices to which they had hitherto been strangers; he appeared to hope that the treaty which removed them to another and a desert country [Oklahoma], would re-establish the ancient organization of the tribes, or at least preserve them in the state in which they now were.

When we arrived at the brow of the hill we perceived the glitter of helmets and swords; troops were drawn up in line along the road. These were not Indians; they were civilized men, sent by the state of Alabama to escort the general. The singular triumphal march to which he had been obliged to submit, now ceased. The Indians saw with some jealousy the American escort range themselves round the general; but we approached the village, and they ran on in order to precede us. We there found them on our arrival, with their garments thrown off, and prepared to afford us a sight of their warlike games.

We arrived on a large plain, around which were situated about an hundred Indian huts, crowned by the rich verdure of the dense thickets; one house was distinguished for its greater size, it was that of the American agent. He also kept an inn, and his wife superintended a school for the instruction of the Indian children. All the men were assembled, deprived of a part of their dress, their faces painted in a grotesque manner, and some wearing feathers in their hair, as a mark of distinction. They then announced to us that there would be a mock fight in honour of their white father. In fact, we soon perceived them separate into two divisions, and form two camps at the two extremities of the place, appoint two leaders, and make preparations for combat. The cry that was uttered by each of these troops, and which we were told was the war-whoop of the Indian tribes, is, perhaps, the most extraordinary modulation of the human voice that can be conceived, and the effect it produced on the combatants of all ages, was still more so. The sport began. They explained the plan to us as follows: Each party endeavoured to drive a ball beyond a certain mark, and that which attained this object seven times would be the victor. We soon saw the combatants, each armed with two long rackets, rush after the light projectile, spring over each other in order to reach it, seize it in the air with incredible dexterity, and hurl it beyond the goal. When the ball was missed by a player, it fell to the ground, when every head was bent, a scene of great confusion ensued, and it was only after a severe struggle that the players succeeded in again throwing it up. In the midst of one of these long combats, whilst all the players were bent around the ball, an Indian detached himself from the group to some distance, returned on a run, sprung into the air, and after making several somersets, threw himself on the shoulders of the other players, leaped into the circle, seized the ball, and for the seventh time cast it beyond the mark. This player was M'Intosh. The victory was obtained by the camp which he commanded; he advanced to receive our congratulations under a shower of applause from a part of the Indian women, whilst the wives of the vanquished appeared to be endeavouring to console them.

The general, after this game, which much amused him, visited the interior of some of the huts, and the Indian school. When we were ready to resume our journey, young M'Intosh re-appeared dressed as an European. He requested permission from the general to accompany him to Montgomery, where he wished to carry his brother, who was about ten years of age, in order to place him under the care of a citizen of Alabama, who had generously offered to educate him. The general consented to it, and we all set out for Uchee Creek, an American tavern, situated on the banks of a creek of that name. We arrived at that place at an early hour, and visited the neighbourhood, which was charming. Accompanied by M'Intosh, I soon made an acquaintance with the Indians of that district. We found them exercising with the bow. I wished to try my skill, M'Intosh likewise armed himself; he had the arm and eye of William Tell. Some proofs of his skill would scarcely be credited were I to relate them. I was most struck with the skill, with which, whilst lying on the ground, he discharged an arrow, which, striking the ground at a few paces distance, made a slight rebound, and flew to an immense distance. This is the mode employed by the Indians when they wish to discharge their arrows to a great distance without discovering themselves. I tried in vain to accomplish it; each time my arrow, instead of rebounding, buried itself in the earth.

We returned to Uchee Creek, and met an Indian chief on his way to the tavern. He was on horseback, with a woman behind him. When he arrived within a few paces of the house, he dismounted and went forward to salute the general, and to make some purchases. During this time his wife remained with the horse, brought it to him when he wished to depart, held the bridle and stirrup when he mounted, and afterwards sprung up behind him. I asked my companions if this woman was the wife of the Indian, and if such was the condition of the females of the nation. They replied, that in general they were treated as we had seen; in the agricultural districts they cultivated the ground, among the hunters they carried the game, the culinary utensils, and other necessary articles, and thus loaded could travel great distances, that even maternal cares scarcely exonerated them from these laborious occupations. However, in the excursions I afterwards made in the environs of Uchee Creek, the condition of the women did not appear to me as unhappy as I was led to expect. I saw before almost all the houses the women sitting in circles, engaged in weaving baskets or mats, and amusing themselves with the games and exercises of the young men, and I never remarked any signs of harshness on the part of the men, or of servile dependence on the part of the women. I was so hospitably received in all the Indian cabins at Uchee Creek, and the country around was so beautiful, that it yet appears to me as the most beautiful spot I ever visited. From Uchee Creek to the cabin of Big Warrior, which is the nearest resting place, is about a day's journey, through a country inhabited by Indians. We several times met parties of them, and were greatly assisted by them in extricating ourselves from dangerous places in

the road, for the storm had encumbered them, and swelled the
streams. On one of these occasions, the general received a touch-
ing specimen of the veneration these sons of nature held him in.
One of the torrents we were to cross had risen above the unnailed
wooden bridge over which the carriage of the general was to proceed. What was our astonishment, on arriving at the stream, to
find a score of Indians, who, holding each other by the hand, and
breast deep in water, marked the situation of the bridge by a double
line. We were well pleased at receiving this succour, and the only
recompense demanded by the Indians, was to have the honour of
taking the general by the hand, whom they called their white father, the envoy of the Great Spirit, the great warrior from France,
who came in former days to free them from the tyranny of the
English. M'Intosh, who interpreted their discourse to us, also expressed to them the general's and our own good wishes. The village of the Big Warrior is thus named on account of the extraordinary courage and great stature of the Indian who was its chief. We
arrived there at a late hour; the chief had been dead some time; the
council of old men had assembled to name his successor, and had
designated one of his sons, remarkable for the same strength of
body, as worthy of filling his place. This son had much conversation with Mr. George Lafayette; he expressed himself in English,
and astonished us by the singular apathy with which he spoke of
the death of his father. But the Indians have not the slightest idea
of what we call grief and mourning. Death does not appear an evil
to them, either as regards the person who has quitted this life, or
those who are thus separated from him. The son of Big Warrior
only appeared to regret that the death of his father, which had occurred a short time before, did not permit him to dispose of his
inheritance, and to present one of the dresses of this celebrated
chief to the general.

We only passed one night with the family of Big Warrior; the
next day we arrived at Line Creek, that is to say, at the frontier of
the Indian country. We were received there by an American who
had married the daughter of a Creek chief, and had adopted the
Indian mode of life. He was a Captain Lewis, formerly in the army

of the United States; his house was commodious, and was furnished with elegance for an Indian cabin. Captain Lewis, who is distinguished for his knowledge and character, appeared to us to exercise great influence over the Indians; he had assembled a great number, well armed and mounted, to act as an escort to the general. One of the neighbouring chiefs came at the head of a deputation to compliment the general. His discourse, which appeared studied, was rather long, and was translated to us by an interpreter. He commenced by high eulogiums on the skill and courage the general had formerly displayed against the English; the most brilliant events of that war was recalled and recounted in a poetical and somewhat pompous strain. He terminated somewhat in these words: "Father, we had long since heard that you had returned to visit our forests and our cabins; you, whom the Great Spirit formerly sent over the great lake to destroy those enemies of man, the English, clothed in bloody raiment. Even the youngest amongst us will say to their descendants, that they have touched your hand and seen your figure, they will also behold you, for you are protected by the Great Spirit from the ravages of age—you may again defend us if we are attacked."

The general replied, through the interpreter, to these compliments of the Indians; he again counselled them to be prudent and temperate; recommended their living in harmony with the Americans, and to always consider them as their friends and brothers; he told them that he should always think of them, and would pray for the welfare of their families and the glory of their warriors. We now directed our course to the stream which separates the Creek country from the state of Alabama. The Indians under Captain Lewis, mounted on small horses as light and nimble as deer, some armed with bows and arrows, and others with tomahawks, followed us in a long file, the rear of which was hidden in the darkness of the forest. On arriving at the brink of the stream, they turned back, uttering loud cries; some of the chiefs, however, bid us a final adieu as we left their territory.

We passed the night on the banks of Line Creek, in a small village of the same name, almost entirely inhabited by persons whom the love of gain had assembled from all parts of the globe, in the midst of these deserts, to turn to their own profit the simplicity and above all the new wants of the unfortunate natives. These avaricious wretches, who without scruple poison the tribes with intoxicating liquors, and afterwards ruin them by duplicity and overreaching, are the most cruel and dangerous enemies of the Indian nations, whom, at the same time, they accuse of being robbers, idlers, and drunkards. If the limits to which I had determined to restrain my narrative had not already been overstepped, I could easily show, that these vices with which they reproach the children of the forest, are the result of the approach of civilization, and also in how many instances they are surpassed by the whites in cruelty and want of faith. I will content myself with citing but two facts from the thousands, which are an eternal stigma on men so proud of the whiteness of their skin, and who call themselves civilized.

A short time since, a trader, living in the state of Alabama, went into the Creek country for the purposes of his business. Having met with one of the chiefs of the nation, he bargained with him for peltries; but, as the conditions he proposed were all disadvantageous to the Indian, to induce him the more readily to consent to them, he intoxicated him with whiskey. After the bargain was concluded, they set out together for the nearest village. On the way, the Indian reflected on what he had done, and perceived that he had been duped; he wished to enter into some other arrangement with the trader, but the discussion soon caused a violent quarrel, which ended by the Indian striking his adversary so violent a blow with his tomahawk, as to stretch him dead at his feet. Twenty-four hours afterwards, on the first complaint of the whites, the murderer was arrested by his own tribe, who, after having assembled their great council, pronounced him guilty of a base assassination, in thus having killed a white who was without arms or means of defence. They then conducted him to the banks of Line Creek; where they had requested the whites to assemble to witness the justice they rendered them, and shot him in their presence.

The evening of our arrival at Line Creek, I went into a store to make some purchases, and whilst there, an Indian entered and asked for twelve and a half cents worth of whiskey. The owner of the shop received the money, and told him to wait a moment, as the concourse of buyers was very great. The Indian waited patiently for a quarter of an hour, after which he demanded his whiskey. The trader appeared astonished, and told him if he wanted whiskey he must first pay him for it. "I gave you twelve and a half cents a few moments since," said the Indian. The poor wretch had scarcely pronounced these words, when the trader sprung forward, seized him by the ears, and, assisted by one of his men, brutally turned him out of the shop. I saw him give the money, and was convinced of the honesty of the one and the rascality of the other. I felt strongly indignant, and notwithstanding the delicacy of my situation, I would have stept forward to interfere, but the whole scene passed so rapidly that I hardly had time to say a few words. I went out to see what the Indian would do. I found him a few steps from the house, where he had been checked by his melancholy emotions. An instant afterwards, he crossed his arms on his breast, and hurried towards his own country with rapid strides. When he arrived on the margin of the stream, he plunged in and crossed it without appearing to perceive that the water reached above his knees. On attaining the other side, he stopped, turned round, and elevating his eyes towards heaven, he extended his hand towards the territory of the whites, in a menacing manner, and uttered some energetic exclamations in his own language. Doubtless, at that moment he invoked the vengeance of heaven on his oppressors; a vengeance that would have been just, but his prayer was in vain. Poor Indians! you are pillaged, beaten, poisoned or excited by intoxicating liquors, and then you are termed savages! [President George] Washington said, "Whenever I have been called upon to decide between an Indian and a white man, I have always found that the white had been the aggressor." Washington was right.

The conduct of the American government is of an entirely different character, as regards the Indian tribes. It not only protects them against individual persecution, and sees that the treaties made with them by the neighbouring states are not disadvantageous to them, and are faithfully adhered to, but it also provides for their wants with a paternal solicitude. It is not a rare circumstance for congress to vote money and supplies to those tribes, whom a deficient harvest or unforeseen calamity have exposed to famine.

We quitted Line Creek on the 3d of April, and the same day General Lafayette was received at Montgomery, by the inhabitants of that village, and by the governor of the state of Alabama, who had come from Cahawba with all his staff and a large concourse of citizens, who had assembled from great distances to accompany him. We passed the next day at Montgomery, and left it on the night of the 4th and 5th, after a ball, at which we had the pleasure of seeing Chilli M'Intosh dance with several beautiful women, who certainly had little idea that they were dancing with a savage. The parting of M'Intosh with the general was a melancholy one. He appeared overwhelmed with sinister presentiments. After having quitted the general and his son, he met me in the courtyard; he stopped, placed my right arm on his, and elevating his left hand towards heaven, "Farewell," said he, "always accompany our father and watch over him. I will pray to the Great Spirit also to watch over him, and give him a speedy and safe return to his children in France. His children are our brothers; he is our father. I hope that he will not forget us." His voice was affected, his countenance sad, and the rays of the moon falling obliquely on his dark visage, gave a solemnity to his farewell with which I was deeply moved. I wished to reply to him, but he quitted me precipitately and disappeared.

4

Bernard,
Duke of Saxe-Weimar-Eisenach
January 1826
⚜

ALTHOUGH BORN IN WEIMAR, CARL BERNHARD, DUKE OF SAXE-WEIMAR-EISENACH (1792-1862) SERVED IN THE OFFICER CORPS OF THE KING OF THE NETHERLANDS. FROM 1806 TO 1815 HE FOUGHT IN THE MAJOR CAMPAIGNS AGAINST NAPOLEON, AND WAS PROMOTED TO LIEUTENANT GENERAL IN 1831. DURING A LEAVE OF ABSENCE IN 1825-26, HE VISITED THE MAJOR CANADIAN AND AMERICAN CITIES. HIS TWO VOLUME ACCOUNT OF THIS VISIT INDICATES THAT HE WAS A CAREFUL AND ASTUTE OBSERVER.

Bernard, Duke of Saxe-Weimar-Eisenach. *Travels through North America during the Years 1825 and 1826.* Philadelphia: Carey, Lea and Carey, 1828. Volume II, pages 26-31.

We passed the river Chatahouchee at one of the ferries belonging to the Indians, and kept in order by them. The right bank is somewhat steep, of red earth, which, from the violent rain, had become slippery. Half a mile from the ferry brought us to Fort Mitchel. It stood upon a height, and was situated to the right of us. We dismounted not far from this, between Indian wigwams at Crowell's tavern. The host was a brother of the Indian agent. This house has also a plantation attached to it, as the one above-mentioned had. Colonel Wool and I were lodged in an airy out-house of clap-boards, without a ceiling, and windows without glass. We were accommodated with freer circulation than would have fallen to our lot in a

German barn. Four companies of the fourth regiment of infantry, the staff of which was fixed at Pensacola, lay in garrison at the fort. The commandant, Major Donoho, and his officers had taken board at Crowell's tavern; in the evening we made acquaintance with them. The most of these officers, pupils of the school at West Point, were men of information, and we passed the remainder of the evening much pleased with their society.

We made the 31st of December [1825] a day of rest, as Colonel Wool had to inspect the garrison of the fort. The four companies here stationed form properly the garrison of Pensacola, and were only sent here last summer during the contest between Georgia and the United States, to protect the Creeks against the encroachments of that State. It openly wishes to take possession of the Indian territory to the Chatahouchee, to which river, agreeable to the charter, Georgia extends. The right bank of the river, on which we now found ourselves, is in the jurisdiction of the State of Alabama. The troops arriving, at first encamped here, but immediately commenced building a new but smaller fort, on the spot where Fort Mitchell stands, so called in honour of the then governor of Georgia, which they now occupy. They hoped, however, that they should return to Pensacola as soon as the disagreements had been settled.

After the inspection, we took a walk to a plantation lying near, which belonged to an Indian named [Chillie] M'Intosh. He was absent at Washington as a delegate from his nation. He is the son of that [William] M'Intosh, who obtained from the State of Georgia the title of General, and who last spring, on account of the treaty with the state, had been shot by his countrymen and hewed in pieces. Polygamy prevails among the Indians. The young M'Intosh had indeed only two wives, a white woman and an Indian. They say he had several wives whom he wished to keep: the white woman however, had driven them with scolding and disgrace out of the house, as she would only submit to one Indian rival. We did not see the Indian wife. The white wife, however, received us quite politely. She is the daughter of a planter in Georgia, and tolerably pretty. She was attired in the European style, only according to the Indian fancy in dress, she carried a quantity of glass beads about her neck. She showed us her two children, completely white, and also the portrait of her father-in-law, as large as life, with the sword of honour given him by the United States. The family is in very good circumstances, and possesses seventy negroes.

In the afternoon we went to a Methodist mission, one short mile distant. We found none but the women at home. The missionaries have established a school, which is frequented by thirty children. They have three Indian girls, boarders, who were extremely modest. The mission is situated in a handsome plantation, on which I saw tame deer. The deer here are evidently smaller than those in Europe.

Sunday, the 1st of January, 1826, we were awakened by the drums and fifes, which announced the new year, by playing Hail Columbia and Yankee Doodle. With the break of day, between seven and eight o-'clock, we left Fort Mitchel, and road twenty-five miles to a plantation called Lewis's, which is located on the spot, upon which, in the last war, Fort Bainbridge stood. The road ran through a very hilly country. At first the soil was sandy and poor, it bore nothing but pine trees. After we had passed over half the distance, the soil improved, it looked reddish-yellow, and the apparently everlasting pines gave place to handsome oaks and lofty hickories. On the other hand the carriage road became very bad, and in a narrow place we upset. The carriage fell slowly towards my side, I took the right moment, sprung from the box on which I sat, and fell upon my feet. This was the eighth time I had been overturned, and never did I escape so cheap as on this occasion. As none of the other gentlemen were injured, we could happily laugh at our accident. The carriage was somewhat damaged, and since we were only four miles distant from Lewis's, and had very fine weather, a true spring day, with clear dark-blue sky, we went the rest of the way on foot.

We passed several wigwams and temporary Indian huts, in which the men lived with the hogs, and lay around the fire with them. A hut of this description is open in front, behind it is closed with pieces of wood and bark. The residents live on roasted venison and Indian corn. The hides of the deer, and even of cattle, they stretch out to dry in the sun, and then sell them. At one hut, covered with cane leaves, there was venison roasting, and bacon smoking. The venison is cut in pieces, and spitted on a cane stalk, many such stalks lie upon two blocks near each other. Under these the fire is kindled, and the stalk continually turned round, till the flesh is dried through. Upon this is laid a hurdle made of cane which rests on four posts. To this are all the large pieces suspended. The hams of bacon are laid upon the hurdle so that the smoke may draw through them.

The grass in many parts of the woods was in a blaze, and many pine trees were burning. We crossed two small streams, the Great and Little Uchee, on tolerable wooden bridges. Between three and four o'clock in the afternoon we reached Lewis's, a handsome house, the best that we had found in the Indian territory. We took here an excellent dinner. We ate daily of the best of venison. In Fort Mitchel we had eaten partridges, of which the officers in one day took fifty-seven in the morning, and forty-six in the evening, in their nets. For the singularity of the thing, I will notice our dinner of to-day, that the inquisitive reader may observe that one is in no danger of hunger on the lands of the Indians: soup of turnips, roast-beef, a roast-turkey, venison with a kind of sour sauce, roast-chickens, and pork with sweet potatoes.

On the 2d of January we rode thirty-one miles to Walker's, also a solitary plantation. The country hilly, the road bad to such a degree that we could only creep along in the most tedious manner, and were obliged to proceed on foot very often. The wood on the other hand grew better and better, and consisted, besides the pines, of handsome oaks, and various sorts of nut-bearing trees, mostly hickories: the soil, for the most part, of a reddish yellow. In several marshy places, and on the banks of rivulets, we saw again the evergreen trees and bushes, and in a swamp nearly a mile long, through which a causeway ran, some magnolia grandiflora which were at least sixty feet high. I also saw here again several trees, which first forming one trunk, four or five feet above the ground, divided themselves into two trunks, and then shot up into the air one hundred feet. In the north-western part of the state of New York, I have seen trees which ran up in five, six, and even seven trunks. Over a stream with marshy banks, a bridge was thrown, three hundred and eleven paces long: the view which I took from this bridge of the luxuriant exotic vegetation which surrounded me, exhibited, as I thought, the original of the sketches of the Brazilian forests in the travels of the Prince Nieuwied. The beautiful day, the cloudless dark-blue sky, also introduced by him, were recalled to me by this picture. But when I observed upon the trees the hateful Spanish moss, I was reminded that I was in the neighbourhood of Columbia and Charleston, and that it was a token of unwholesome air. In the swamps I noticed several plants which were known to me from hot-house cultivation, but unfortunately I cannot recall their names.

The country is comparatively populously inhabited by Indians. They live partly in wigwams, partly in bark cabins. Before one of these huts, or cabins, hung a skinned otter, upon which they seemed preparing to make a meal. The Indians roast their maize on the naked coals, then they throw it into a cavity made in a trunk of a tree, and pound it with a stick of wood into a sort of coarse meal. I bought a species of nuts, which were roasted, ground-nuts, and amused myself with the propensity to thievery a young Indian displayed. As I was putting the nuts in my pocket, one or more would drop, instantly the young fellow would step forward, as if by accident, set his foot on the nut, take it between his toes, and move off. We passed through a tolerably cleared, fenced, and built district, in which several negro quarters of a decent appearance were scattered about. This plantation belonged to a chief, one of the principal of the Creeks, called the Big Warrior, who owns above three hundred negroes, whose wooden dwelling-house stands in the centre of his property. He is now at Washington, as one of the deputies of his nation. We came over another cleared spot, where the Indians were routed in the last war by the Georgia militia under General Floyd.

Not far from this place, we noticed a number of Indians collected in the neighbourhood of a plantation. We left our carriage to inquire into the cause of it. There had been a horse race of middling unsightly horses: the festival was, however, ended, and the meeting was on the point of breaking up. A white planter who was there, conducted us to the son of the Big Warrior. He was himself a chief, and possessed a high reputation, as was said amongst those of the nation. He sat upon a felled tree between two inferior chiefs. His dress was a tunic of flowered, clear blue calico, a piece of the same stuff was wrapped round his head like a turban. He wore richly ornamented leather leggings set with glass beads, and mocassins, and had an equally ornamented hunting pouch hung around him. Moderately fat, and of a great stature, he appeared to be about thirty years old. He had mustaches like all his country-men. I was introduced to him, and shook hands with him. The conversation was very trifling and short. It took place through an interpreter who appeared to be a dismissed soldier. This creature caused the chief to rise when we commenced speaking to him; when I begged him to remain sitting, he reseated himself mechani-cally. He directed no questions to me, and answered mine with yes and no. To the question, whether he knew any thing of the country of which I was a native, he answered by a shake of the head. He looked no more at me. Several Indians wore their hair in a singu-lar style; it was shorn on both sides of the head, and the middle, from the neck over to the forehead, stood up like a cock's comb. Seen from behind, they appeared as if they wore a helmet. Quite small boys practised themselves already in shooting with a little bow. I attempted to joke with a little fellow, three years old, but he took the jest in bad part, and threatened me with his bow.

After sunset, towards six o'clock in the evening, we reached Walker's, and found a good reception in a large log-house, each of us had a separate chamber. The landlord was a captain of infantry in the United States' service formerly, and had, as our host of yes-terday, an Indian wife.

On the following day we rode to Montgomery, twenty-five miles distant. The road was in the beginning bad, afterwards, how-ever, really good. We crossed a bridge over a stream one hundred paces long, and were then obliged to toil over a long, wretched causeway. The vegetation was again exceedingly luxuriant, it was remarkably beautiful on the banks of Line Creek, a little river, which forms the boundary between the Indian territory and the state of Alabama, eight miles from Walker's. Very lofty live oaks, and oaks of other descriptions, several magnolias, and amongst them, a particularly handsome and lofty macrophylla.

As we entered upon the territory of Alabama, we soon observed that we were upon a much better soil. It was darker, much wood was removed, and signs of cultivation every where. Upon several plantations, the cotton fields exhibited themselves in beautiful order; the log houses were only employed as negro cabins; the mansion-houses, two stories high, are for the most part painted white, and provided with piazzas and balconies. At most of them the cotton gins and presses were at work. The planters had not finished the whole of their crop, on account of the unusual drought. The Alabama river was so low that the steam-boats had not been able for several weeks to pass from Mobile to Montgomery. This place had therefore, for a length of time, suffered for the want of the most necessary supplies, which are drawn from Mobile; fifteen dollars had been asked for one bushel of salt. We met several caravans of emigrants from the eastern part of Georgia, who were on their way to Butler county, Alabama, to settle themselves on land which they had purchased very cheap from the United States. The number of their negroes, wagons, horses, and cattle, showed that these emigrants were in easy circumstances. On account of the bad road, we went at first a good deal on foot; at one of the creeks, the carriage passed through the ford, and we footmen crossed over on one of the simplest bridges in the world, namely, a felled pine tree of great size. We arrived at Montgomery about two o'clock. In the night it had frozen, but the day had solaced us with the warmth of spring.

5

Basil Hall
April 1828
❦

S COTTISH-BORN BASIL HALL (1788-1844) ROSE TO THE RANK OF CAP-
TAIN IN THE ROYAL NAVY FROM WHICH HE RETIRED IN 1823. IN
1818 HE PUBLISHED AN ACCOUNT OF HIS VOYAGE TO KOREA AND THE
RYUKYU ISLANDS. IT, AND A SUBSEQUENT ACCOUNT FIVE YEARS LATER
ON CHILE, PERU AND MEXICO, WERE WELL RECEIVED. IN ADDITION TO
HIS TRAVEL JOURNALS, HE WROTE NOVELS, SHORT STORIES, AND PAPERS
FOR SCIENTIFIC PERIODICALS. HE WAS A FELLOW OF THE ROYAL SOCIETY,
AS WELL AS THE ROYAL ASTRONOMICAL, ROYAL GEOGRAPHICAL, AND
GEOLOGICAL SOCIETIES.

HE PUBLISHED A THREE-VOLUME ACCOUNT OF HIS TRAVELS IN NORTH
AMERICA, WHICH HE MADE WITH HIS WIFE. ON THEIR TOUR, THE HALLS
MET DANIEL WEBSTER, DEWITT CLINTON, WILLIAM ASTOR, AND PRESI-
DENT JOHN QUINCY ADAMS. CAPTAIN HALL'S CANDID CRITICISM OF THE
UNITED STATES, WHICH IRRITATED AMERICAN READERS, REVEALED HIS
BELIEF THAT DEMOCRACY PRODUCES AN INFERIOR SOCIETY.

Basil Hall. *Travels in North America in the Years 1827 and
1828*. 3 vols. Edinburgh: Cadel and Company, 1829. Volume
III, pages 288-307.

On the 1st day of April, 1828, we crossed the river Chatahoochie,
and entered the country of the Creek Indians. At the Agency, and
along the sides of the road, for a considerable distance, we saw
crowds of those miserable wretches who had been dislodged from

their ancient territory to the eastward of the river, but had not yet taken root in the new lands allotted to them. It is true, they had received a pecuniary compensation on the extinction of their titles to the land of their forefathers; yet they were men of far too improvident habits to have brought their new lands into cultivation; and consequently, when their stock of money was expended, they were left in a state bordering on starvation. In similar circumstances, a party of New Englanders would have cleared away the trees, built themselves houses, and the whole right bank of the river, with every other spot of fertile soil, would have been under the plough in half the time. But to these poor Indians, who have lived chiefly by hunting, and whose farming operations were confined to a garden near their huts, the labour of clearing a new country was quite out of the question; and great numbers of them actually perished from want. The United States agent, however, I was glad to see, was assisting them with provisions and clothing, and I have no doubt relieved their distress materially. As we left the Chatahoochie behind us, and travelled through the woods to the westward, we gradually lost sight of that part of the Creek tribe who were wandering about like bees whose hive had been destroyed, and came upon Indians of the same race, who were still allowed to live on the lands which had descended to them from their ancestors.

On the evening of the second day, after leaving Columbus, we reached the house of another of the United States agents, who resides among the Indians, and is one of the channels of communication between them and the government. We could not have arrived at a more fortunate moment, as it was the eve of one of their grand ball-plays; an exhibition, the agent told us, well worth seeing—from its being a perfectly genuine, unsophisticated display of the Indians who had resided on the spot from time immemorial. The play itself was to take place next morning, but our considerate host advised me to see the preparatory ceremonies, and very kindly offered to accompany me to one of their council squares, distant about a league from his house.

It appears, that the inhabitants of one Indian village always play against those of another, and as these games are not mere

Embryo Town of Columbus on the Chatahoochie
From a Camera Lucida drawing by Basil Hall

matters of sport, but the chief object of their lives, a great deal of
ceremony and many previous arrangements are necessary.

The moon rose when we were about half way to the scene
where the Indians were assembled. The night was bright and frosty,
and so perfectly still that we could hear the shrill cries of the savages, and the thumpings of their barbarous music, at the distance
of more than a mile. The pine barren, seen by moonlight, had a
very striking appearance; and so had one of the Indian villages
through which we passed. It consisted of about twenty log huts,
each of them guarded by a brace of dogs, which, in the absence of
their masters, assembled in a circle round our horses, and made us
glad enough to pass on.

We found the Indians in a square court, about twenty yards
across, formed by four covered sheds, in which were seated several of the chiefs, and more than a hundred of the other natives. In
each of these sheds there was erected a raised shelf or floor, about
a foot and a half from the ground, dipping towards the court, and
covered by a smooth, hard mat, made of split canes, sewed together. On this the principal Indians were seated in state, cross-
legged, or stretched, with equal dignity, at their full length.

In the middle of the court blazed an immense fire of pitch-pine wood, the light from which, added to that of the moon, which was now well up, made every thing quite distinct. Round the fire sat, or rather squatted, about a dozen elderly Indians—none of them much encumbered with clothing—smoking pipes, which they handed from one to the other, laughing and shouting with great animation, and turning back from time to time to speak to another circle of younger men, who were standing near enough to warm themselves, or even to reach over the heads of the seniors to catch up a piece of burning timber to light their pipes with.

On one side of the illuminated square, in the front part of the shed, sat two musicians, one of them was hammering away with his fingers on a drum, formed of a piece of deer-skin stretched over a hollowed trunk of a tree, while the other kept time with a large gourd containing a handful of gravel. In the square itself, and fronting the shed, which contained this primitive orchestra, twenty squaws, or female Indians, were ranged in a semi-circle, with their backs to the rest of the company—such being, I suppose, the fashionable etiquette amongst the Creeks. As these ladies never once turned round their faces, I am saved the delicate task of describing their looks. Their dance, however, if the very slight movements of their feet and bodies could be so called, was merely a sort of wriggle of the body; but, as the whole party kept excellent time in these movements, it had a most ludicrous appearance. At every fourth or fifth bar, they all struck in with a short, faint, sharp cry, of a particularly wild, and, I thought, somewhat mournful sound. These damsels wore no head-dress, but allowed their black, oily hair to hang down upon their necks and shoulders, over which was thrown, most decorously, a gaudy cotton shawl—weaved for aught I know in Manchester or Paisley.

I was sitting beside the principal chief, and thinking the scene rather dull, which he perhaps suspected, when he uttered a few words of command. In a moment about thirty young Indians flew to the side of the court, where each of them snatched up a couple of the sticks or bats used in the ball-play afterwards to be described. After marshalling themselves for a minute or two, they rushed forward again like so many demons, till they formed a circle round the fire, yelling, screaming, and shouting all the time, in the most terrible way, tumbling heels over head, performing various antics, and waving their sticks, as if they had been frantic. I have no idea of any thing being more completely savage, nor shall I soon forget the way in which their shrieks pierced through and through my head.

After this exhibition was over, torches were ordered, and I was invited by another of the chiefs to adjourn to a neighbouring building, an immense hut of a flat, sugar-loaf shape, rising in the centre to the height of at least thirty feet, and measuring about sixty or perhaps eighty feet across the floor. It had no wall, as the roof, which was thatched, reached to the ground. A circular seat, skirting the inside, ten feet broad, touched the roof all the way round. In the middle of the sandy floor a fire was burning, round which were assembled some of the most athletic young men of the village, who had been previously selected by the elders as performers in the next day's sport.

These youths were not long in stripping off all their clothes, except a slight wrapper round the middle. I could see at once, that something remarkable was about to take place, but what it was I could not conjecture. Their first operation was to tie cords tightly round one another's arms and thighs, so as effectually to check the course of the blood in the veins. As soon as this was done, they splashed themselves over with water from head to foot, and then very deliberately allowed their limbs to be scratched or rather scarified by some old Indians, who attended for that purpose with instruments, the name of which I forget. Some of these were made of common needles stuck in a piece of wood, but those most in fashion were formed out of the teeth of the fish called Gar. I purchased one of them, which is now in my possession; it consists of two rows, one of fifteen, the other of fourteen sharp teeth, tied firmly, by means of a grass fibre, to the core of the maize, or to what is called in America a corn-cob.

Each of the young Indians, who was to be operated upon, placed himself in a sloping position against one of the wooden pillars which supported the roof, clasping it with his hands. The experienced performers then drew the instrument I have just described, apparently as hard as he could press it, along the arms and legs of these resolute fellows, over a space of about nine inches in length, so that each of the teeth cut into the skin, or, at all events, made a very decided mark, or furrow, along the surface. The sharp sound of these scrapings was very disagreeable to the ear.

Five separate scratchings were made on each man's leg below the knee, five on each thigh, and five on each arm; in all, thirty sets of cuts. As the instrument contained about thirty teeth, each Indian must in every case have had several hundred lines drawn on his skin. The blood flowed profusely as long as the bandages were kept tight. This, indeed, seemed to be one of their principal objects, as the Indians endeavoured to assist the bleeding by throwing their arms and legs about, holding them over, and sometimes placing them almost in, the fire, for a second or two. It was altogether a hideous and frightful scene. For my own part, I scarcely knew how to feel when I found myself amongst some dozens of naked savages, streaming with blood from top to toe, skipping and yelling round a fire, or talking at the top of their voices in a language of which I knew nothing, or laughing as merrily as if it were the best fun in the world to be cut to pieces. Not one of these lads uttered the slightest complaint during the operation; but when I watched their countenances closely, I observed that only two or three bore the discipline without shrinking or twisting their faces a little.

I was told that these scarifications and bleedings rendered the men more limber and active, and bring them into proper condition to undergo the exertion of the ball-play on the following morning. I don't know how this may be with my friends the Creeks; but I suspect half a dozen of the cuts, of which each of these young fellows received some hundreds, would have laid me up for a week!

Next day, at nine o'clock, on the 3d of April, we set out for the scene of this famous Indian game; and, after wandering about for some time, we found the spot in the bosom of the forest, at the distance of a mile or two from the road. It consisted of an open space about 200 yards in length by 20 yards wide, from which the trees had been cleared away, though the grass was left untouched, nor was the surface even levelled. At each end of this area two green boughs were thrust into the ground, six feet apart from each other, as a sort of wicket. The object of the game, it afterwards appeared, was to drive the ball between these boughs; and which-ever party succeeded in accomplishing this, counted one.

As the natives had reported that the play would begin at ten o'clock, we hurried to the ground; but when we got there we could discover no symptoms of business, not a soul was to be seen, and we had the whole forest to ourselves. In process of time a few straggling Indians joined us; but it was fully three hours after the time specified before the contending parties made their appear-ance. I have regretted ever since that I did not employ this interval in sketching some of these most elegant groups with the Camera Lucida, but, until it was all over, this never once occurred to me; and thus I let slip the only opportunity which the whole journey— I may say my whole life—presented of drawing these interesting savages in a leisurely way.

By one o'clock the surrounding space was thickly speckled over with Creek women, accompanied by numerous squads of copper-coloured little Creekies; but still the real parties in the con-test were nowhere to be seen.

From time to time, indeed, we had sufficient indications of their being somewhere in the neighbourhood, from the loud shrieks or yells raised by a great number of voices in chorus, which issued from the forest, sometimes on one side, and sometimes on the other; but not a soul was yet visible. The agent and I, being tempted to walk, upon one occasion, in the direction of these cries, came to an opening where some forty or fifty naked savages were lying flat on the grass, seemingly in a state of listlessness, or fatigue from the preceding night's dissipation. On moving a little further on, we came to various parties at their toilet. Some of these dan-dies of the woods were busily employed in painting one eye black, the other yellow. Several youths, more wealthy than the rest, I suppose, were thrusting long black feathers into their turbans, or cloths which they had wound round their heads, much in the style of Orientals. Others were fitting their naked bodies with tails, to resemble tigers and lions, having already daubed and streaked them-selves over from head to foot with a variety of colours, intended to set off the coppery tinge of their own red skins—anxious that art might co-operate as far as possible with nature, in making them look as much like wild beasts as possible.

At last, a far louder cry than we had yet heard burst from the woods in the opposite direction. Upon looking up, we saw the Indians of the other party advancing to the ball play ground in a most tumultuous manner, shrieking, yelling, hallooing, brandishing their sticks, performing somersets, and exhibiting all conceivable antics. At this stage of the game, I was forcibly reminded of the pictures in Cook's Voyages, where multitudes of the South Sea Islanders are represented as rushing forward to attack the boats. This resemblance was heightened by the similarity of the dress, or rather of the undress; for, with the exception of an occasional wrapper across the brow, and a small, square, dark-coloured cloth, about one quarter as big as a pocket handkerchief, tied by a slender cord round the middle, most of them were exactly as Dame Nature turned them out of hand.

There were fifty of the inhabitants of one village pitted against fifty of another; and the players, being selected from the strongest, nimblest, and most spirited of the whole tribe, the party offered some of the finest specimens of the human form I ever beheld. While waiting for the appointed time of action, the natives stretched themselves on the grass, or stood with their arms folded, or leaned against the trees; but all of them unconsciously fell into attitudes of such perfect ease and gracefulness, as would have enchanted the heart of a painter.

Heretofore I had hardly ever seen Indians, except lounging about on the roadsides, wrapped in dirty blankets, begging for tobacco, or stealing, like strange dogs, timorously, and more than half tipsy, through the streets. At all events, I had so little idea that the race was possessed either of activity or of any beauty of form, that had I been asked, the day before this ball-play, what I thought of the Indians in these respects, I might have answered, that they are all bow-legged, slouchy, ungraceful, and inactive. Whereas, in point of fact, the very reverse of all this is true.

The first party, on rushing out of the woods in the manner I have described, danced, in the same noisy and tumultuous fashion, round the two green boughs at their end of the ground. After this first explosion, they advanced more leisurely to the middle of the cleared space, where they squatted down in a thick cluster till their antagonists made their appearance. The same ceremonies were observed by the second party, after which they settled down likewise on the grass in a body. The two groups remained eyeing one another for a long time, occasionally uttering yells of defiance.

At a signal from one of the chiefs, the two parties suddenly sprung to their feet, and stood brandishing their sticks over their heads. Every player held one of these implements in each hand. They were formed of light, tough wood, I think willow, about two feet long, and as thick as my thumb. At the end farthest from the hand, the sticks were split and formed into an oval, three inches long by two wide, across which opening, or loop, were stretched two thongs made of hide. By means of these bats, the ball was struck to a great distance whenever any of the players succeeded in hitting it fairly. This, however, was not very often the case, for reasons which will be stated immediately. Generally speaking, the ball was grasped or held between the ends of the two sticks, and carried along over the head by the fortunate player who had got hold of it. The ball was pretty much like that used in Tennis courts, only not so hard, being formed out of raw hide stuffed with deer's hair.

After the parties had stood for some minutes in silence, in two rows facing one another, they stepped forward till they came within the distance of a few feet. Upon some word of command being given by one of the chiefs, every one laid down his sticks before him on the ground. A deputation of the chiefs highest in rank now proceeded to examine and count the parties, in order to make sure of there being an equal number on both sides. All these ceremonies, and various others which I forget, being ended, an old man stood forward and made a speech, or talk, as it is called, which, being interpreted to us, appeared to be formed of injunctions to the combatants to observe fair play, and to do honour to their country upon this important occasion. As soon as he ceased, the Indians scattered themselves over the ground, according to some rules not unlike those of cricket, by which the players might intercept the ball, and send it back again in the right direction. I observed that each of the goals, or wickets, formed by the two boughs at the ends, was guarded by a couple of the most expert players, whose duty it was to prevent the ball passing through the opening—the especial object of their antagonists.

These long-protracted ceremonials and preparations being over, one of the chiefs, having advanced to the centre of the area, cast the ball high in the air. As it fell, between twenty and thirty of the players rushed forward, and, leaping several feet off the ground, tried to strike it. The multiplicity of blows, acting in different directions, had the effect of bringing the ball to the ground, where a fine scramble took place, and a glorious clatter of sticks mingled with the cries of the savages. At length an Indian, more expert than the others, contrived to nip the ball between the ends of his two sticks, and, having managed to fork it out, ran off with it like a deer, with his arms raised over his head, pursued by the whole party engaged in the first struggle. The fortunate youth was, of course, intercepted in his progress twenty different times by his antagonists, who shot like hawks across his flight from all parts of the field, to knock the prize out of his grasp, or to trip him up—in short, by any means to prevent his throwing it through the opening between the boughs at the end of the play-ground. Whenever this grand purpose of the game was accomplished, the successful party announced their right to count one by a fierce yell of triumph, which seemed to pierce the very depths of the wilderness. It was sometimes highly amusing to see the way in which the Indian who had got hold of the ball contrived to elude his pursuers. It is not to be supposed he was allowed to proceed straight to the goal, or wicket, or even to get near it; but, on the contrary, he was obliged, in most cases, to make a circuit of many hundred yards amongst the trees, with thirty or forty swift-footed fellows stretching after or athwart him, with their fantastic tigers' tails streaming behind them; and he, in like manner, at full speed, holding his sticks as high over his head as possible, sometimes ducking to avoid a blow, or leaping to escape a trip, sometimes doubling like a hare, and sometimes tumbling at full length, or breaking his shins on a fallen tree, but seldom losing hold of his treasure without a severe struggle. It really seemed as if the possessor of the ball upon these occasions had a dozen pair of eyes, and was gifted for the time with double speed; for, in general, he had not only to evade the attacks of those who were close to him, but to avoid being cut off, as it is called in nautical language, by the others farther ahead. These parts of the game were exciting in the highest degree, and it almost made the spectators breathless to look at them.

Sometimes the ball, when thrown up in the first instance by the chief, was reached and struck by one of the party before it fell to the ground. On these occasions, it was driven far amongst the pine-trees, quite out of sight to our eyes, but not to those of the Indians, who darted towards the spot, and drove it back again. In general, however, they contrived to catch the ball before it fell, and either to drive it back, or to grasp it and run along, as I have described, towards the end of the ground. Sometimes they were too eager to make much noise; but whenever a successful blow was made, the people on the winning side uttered a short yell, so harsh and wild, that it made my blood run cold every time I heard it, from being associated with tortures, human sacrifices, scalpings, and all the horrors of Indian warfare.

The notation of the game was most primitive. Two of the oldest and most trustworthy of the chiefs were seated on one side, each with ten small sticks in his hand, one of which was thrust into the sand every time the ball happened to be driven through the wicket. Twenty was game; but I observed these learned sages never counted higher than ten, so that when it became necessary to mark eleven, the whole ten sticks were pulled out, and one of them replaced.

Sometimes the ball fell amongst the groups of lookers on, the women and children of the different Indian villages. It did not signify a straw, however, who was in the way; all respect of persons, age, and sex was disregarded, in the furious rush of the players, whose whole faculties seemed concentrated in the game alone.

The agent had previously taught me the art of avoiding the mischief of these whirlwind rushes of the Indians; and it was fortunate for me that he did so. I was standing on one side of the ground, admiring a grand chase, which was going on at some considerable distance, when one of the players, who was watching his opportunity, intercepted the fugitive, and struck the ball out of the other's grasp, though he was bounding along with it at a prodigious rate. The ball pitched within a yard or two of the spot where I was standing. In the next instant a dozen or twenty Indians whizzed past me, as if they had been projected from cannons. I sprung to the nearest tree, as I had been instructed, and putting my hands and legs round, embraced it will all my might. A poor boy, however, close to me, had not time to imitate my example, and

An American Stage-Coach
From a Camera Lucida drawing by Basil Hall

being overwhelmed by the multitude, was rolled over and over half a dozen times, in spite of his screams, which were lost in the clatter of sticks, and the yells and the shouts of the combatants, who by this time had become animated by the exercise, and were letting out the secret of their savage nature very fast. I felt rather awkward, I must confess, as they rushed against me, and very nearly scraped me off; but I held fast, and escaped with a good daubing of rosin from the pine-tree. In half a minute afterwards the contest was raging some hundreds of yards off.

We did not stay to see the end of the game, as there was danger of our being benighted, an event which happened, however, notwithstanding all our precautions. I have since regretted much that

I did not profit as far as I might have done by this only opportunity I ever had, or am ever likely to have, of seeing the habits of these people, who are fast vanishing from the face of the earth. After the game is over, the agent told me the opposite parties are frequently so much excited, that they fall to in earnest, and try the strength of their sticks on each others' heads. A row in the forest amongst its native inhabitants would have been well worth seeing, and I do not know what induced me to let slip such a chance. An idea often comes across travellers, that what they have actually before them, may be commanded at any time, and accordingly they are much too careless in availing themselves of the means really within their grasp, and lose half their advantages, in the vain expectation of better opportunities arising. Besides which, various other circumstances come into play at these moments to encourage the wanderer's indolence. He may be tired, or hungry, or dispirited, or he may be so entirely out of conceit, as it is called, with the whole journey, and every thing connected with it, that he may wonder why he ever undertook the expedition, and heartily wish it over. At such times all things are seen through a bilious medium of languid indifference, the most fatal of all to energetic observation and research, and of course still more fatal to lively description.

It frequently occurred to me, when looking at this animated game, that it might be introduced with great effect at the public schools in England, and I hope my description may suffice for the purpose of explaining the details. There is no reason, indeed, why the young men of Eton or Harrow should paint one eye green, and the other yellow, or daub their legs and arms with lamp black. Neither is there any thing essential in having a tiger's tail behind, or that their dress should be reduced to the small compass considered fashionable by these worthy Aborigines. Nor, I think, need they consider it right to scarify their limbs with a comb made of fishes' teeth, or to dance all the preceding night round a blazing wood fire in the open air; still less to get drunk on whisky after the game is over—indispensable conditions amongst the Creek Indians in the forests of Alabama.

6

Margaret Hall
April 1828
🪶

MARGARET HALL (1799-1876), DAUGHTER OF SIR JOHN HUNTER, SOME-
TIME BRITISH CONSUL-GENERAL IN SPAIN, MARRIED CAPTAIN BASIL HALL
IN 1825, TWO YEARS AFTER HE RETIRED FROM THE ROYAL NAVY. THEY
HAD TWO DAUGHTERS AND A SON. SHE WAS WIDOWED IN 1844.

As A YOUNG WOMAN AND WIFE OF MERELY THREE YEARS SHE AC-
COMPANIED HER HUSBAND ON A TOUR OF NORTH AMERICA. THE HALLS
BROUGHT THEIR DAUGHTER ELIZA, WHO WAS ABOUT TWO YEARS OLD WHEN
THEY, AND THE CHILD'S NURSE, A MRS. COWNIE, CROSSED THROUGH
CREEK TERRITORY.

CAPTAIN HALL'S ACCOUNT WAS PUBLISHED IN 1829, BUT MRS. HALL'S
LETTERS, WHICH WERE WRITTEN TO HER SISTER JANE WITH NO OTHER
READERS IN MIND, WERE NOT PUBLISHED UNTIL 1931.

Margaret Hall. *The Aristocratic Journey; Being the Outspoken Letters of Mrs. Basil Hall Written during a Fourteenth Months' Sojourn
in America 1827-1828.* Pages 240-244. Una Pope-Hennessey, editor.
Copyright 1930 by Dame Una Pope-Hennessey, renewed copyright
© 1931 by James Pope-Hennessey. Used by permission of G. P.
Putnam's Sons, a division of Penguin Putnam Inc.

LEWIS'S TAVERN, IN THE CREEK NATION, APRIL I
[1828]:—The Indian chiefs allow white men to establish taverns
in their territory for the accommodation of travellers. We are this
night at a most excellent one kept by a man of the name of Lewis,
who has a squaw to wife. We are in a closed house and have got

49

blazing fires, which the change in the weather rendered very necessary. I suffered badly from cold last night, so much, indeed, that I could not sleep, and there was sufficient talking and snoring all round me to keep me awake independently of the change of weather, for we occupied a room containing four beds out of which had been thrust four gentlemen who had to be put up in the little places close to us. Altho' I have groaned over each day's journey with the feeling of one whose every bone aches from ill usage, our longest distance has been very little over thirty miles and more commonly under it, and as there are only certain houses that are tolerably decent to stay at, we are obliged to go on from one to the other, according as we learn which are the usual stopping places of other travellers. Then, too, we are generally so uncomfortable in the house that we are anxious to get out of it as early as possible, tho' we are just as desirous by the end of the day to quit the carriage. In spite of the various discomforts we have experienced, there has been great interest in the journey, but I shall rejoice most truly when we arrive at Montgomery. What I have felt the greatest suffering is the dirt that we have to put up with in everything, even in our food. This is an appearance of dirt that is very disgusting. One thing we have to be thankful for is that we have all enjoyed such perfect health throughout the whole journey, as for Eliza, she is as hardy as a wild Indian and nearly about as wild. She has never caught the slightest cold in spite of all the exposure she has had.

CAPTAIN TRIPLETT'S CABIN, CREEK NATION, APRIL 2:—
We are now within twenty-seven miles of Montgomery, which terminates our land travelling for the present, and it was our intention to have pushed on there very early to-morrow morning, but the landlord here has told us of a ball play that the Indians are to have to-morrow, and as we may not have another opportunity of seeing such a sight we mean to delay our journey a few hours for the purpose of being present at it. They dance all this night previous to the ball play, and Basil is gone with Captain Triplett to see them. Had there been any mode of conveyance for me I should have gone likewise, tho' I am abundantly tired and sleepy.

I think I have mentioned more than once that we were astonished that more questions were not asked of us by the Americans, whose inquisitiveness is so proverbial, but I find that, altho' they do not interrogate us, Mrs. Cownie is bothered to death by their questions and highly indignant at the ignorance and stupidity displayed by many of them. Of course they always ask where we come from and after telling that we are from England, she has been asked whether we have learned to speak English since coming to America. [Passage omitted about Columbus, Georgia.]

MONTGOMERY, STATE OF ALABAMA, APRIL 5:—We are at length at Montgomery, which finishes our land travelling for the present, and in an hour we are to embark on board of the steamboat which is to carry us down the River Alabama to Mobile, a distance of nearly five hundred miles, which we shall be two or three or four days in accomplishing. We are very anxious to have reached Mobile before Easter Sunday, for at Montgomery there is no Episcopal Church, so it was not worth our while remaining here for so many days.

Yesterday morning we remained at Captain Triplett's till we heard the Indians begin to yell in the woods, which was a sign that they were assembling. This was at ten o'clock. The horses were then put to the carriage, and pioneered by our landlord we proceeded about a half a mile through the very heart of the forest and where none but a thoroughly good driver could have ventured to drive a carriage. There we stopped on a little eminence overlooking the valley where the Indians were to play. We were the first persons on the ground and had upwards of two hours to wait before what we went to see commenced, but we were interested by various groups, some of whites in waggons, but mostly of Indian women and children in their best attire, who collected in the mean time. All this time we heard strange yells from the opposite parties, and at length one party rushed on the ground throwing themselves into all sorts of fantastic attitudes, like nothing I ever saw except the plates of Captain Cook's Voyages, and with no more dress on. Their bodies and faces were painted with various colours, they wore feathers in their heads, and some of them tails of beasts.

In short, it is impossible to conceive anything more thoroughly savage, but it was interesting to see such a sight totally unsophisticated by any mixture of civilization, and on the ground that has belonged to the Indians from time immemorial, tho' probably it will not belong to them much longer. The first party then seated themselves on the ground and the others made their appearance in the same manner and garb, or no garb, to speak more correctly. Each party consisted of fifty. The game I cannot pretend to describe, for there was so much danger of being knocked over in the course of their sport that I was advised to retreat into the carriage which was placed at too great a distance for me to be able to judge of anything except the extraordinary agility with which they run, which appears all the more extraordinary when contrasted with their usually very indolent, lounging habits. We remained till two o'clock, and then fearful of being benighted on our way to Montgomery we set off and soon regained the high road. Six miles further on we crossed the Old Line Creek, which divides the Creek Nation from the State of Alabama, and nineteen miles more brought us to Montgomery. The last seven miles it was quite dark and we had to creep along very cautiously as neither the driver not the horses were acquainted with the ruts and other dangers of the road which altho' quite perfect when compared with what we have lately travelled over had still a sufficient number of defects to require careful driving. We got to Montgomery about eight o'clock and learned that a steamboat starts for Mobile to-day.

7

James Stuart

March 1830

❧

SCOTTISH-BORN JAMES STUART (1775-1849) WAS A LAWYER, JUSTICE OF THE PEACE, WHIG POLITICIAN, OFFICER OF HIS COUNTY'S MILITIA, AND NEWSPAPER EDITOR. HIS AFFAIRS SUFFERED AFTER KILLING SIR ALEXANDER BOSWELL IN A DUEL, AND STUART SOON UNDERTOOK A THREE-YEAR TOUR OF THE UNITED STATES. HIS THREE-VOLUME ACCOUNT, WHICH WAS SO WELL RECEIVED AS TO HAVE THREE EDITIONS IN ITS FIRST TWO YEARS, FAVORABLY PRESENTS THE AMERICAN CAUSE.

James Stuart. *Three Years in North America*, Edinburgh: Robert Cadell, 1833. Volume II, pages 157-159, 169-170.

Colonel Colman was the only passenger in the stage when we set off on Monday morning the 15th March [1830], from Fort Mitchell. We dined at a very tolerable country inn, fourteen miles from Fort Mitchell, kept by a person of the name of Royston.

The Indians whom we saw were very civil, giving us presents now and then, when the horses were watered, of the peccan nut. In the evening we stopped at Harris's hotel, near Fort Bainbridge, which is now dismantled. We arrived there early in the afternoon. I was glad to find the hotel more comfortable than that at Fort Mitchell. I secured a single-bedded room as soon as I arrived, and was surprised to find Cowper's poems on a table in the room, while there was not even a pane of glass in the window.

Two persons on horseback reached the hotel soon after us. One of them turned out to be the overseer of a great plantation in the neighbourhood. He represented his situation as very desirable in all respects, excepting the duty which he had to perform of whipping the slaves. He and his fellow traveller, soon after their arrival, got water, and proceeded to wash and shave in the open space between the pens of the dwelling house. Here there was a bench for pewter basins of water; and a very large towel, meant for general use, was hung on a wooden roller, fixed to the side of the wall. I have seen the same sort of washing equipage in the porticos at the back of the house, and in these open spaces in many of the smaller country hotels; but I found little difficulty here, or on former occasions, in procuring a basin of water and towel separately for my own use. Walking out in the evening to see Fort Bainbridge, I met several Indians, who were perfectly kind and good-humoured. One of them did me some mischief unintentionally, by breaking a small pocket thermometer, which I was showing him. From them I learned that Tuskina had been here yesterday, and that he was determined to deliver himself up before the time appointed for his trial,—his object in avoiding being at present taken into custody, was merely that he might not incur the risk of being imprisoned. In the evening the stage from the south came up, and at supper there were no less than ten persons, including an Indian, a very handsome young man, who, we found, was to travel with us on the following day. Mrs. Harris presided at the head of the table, her husband acting as waiter. We had every thing very good, but no wheaten bread. Excellent coffee and tea, venison, fowls, ham, eggs, &c. We breakfasted on the following morning at Walker's house, the last of the hotels in the Creek country, and found good bread and an excellent breakfast. We observed very fine poultry in the neighbourhood, and Guinea and pea-fowls. We found the Indian who accompanied us, and who, with some of the Creeks, had recently been induced to emigrate to the western side of the Mississippi, and had now been on a visit to his old friends, by no means an uninformed person. He is now engaged in agricultural pursuits, but still seemed to regret having left the land of his fathers. He spoke English well, but had not been taught to read so as to make him a proficient. The females among the Creeks he represents as perfectly chaste and virtuous after marriage, but not restricted in their intercourse while unmarried. Widows are prohibited from marrying, and from all sexual intercourse, for four years after the death of the husband; and this regulation is strictly enforced. A plurality of wives is allowed where the husband is possessed of sufficient property to enable him to maintain them. The customs of different tribes of Indians are, *however, essentially different* in these respects. [Stuart digresses for nine pages—as he relates reports of North American Indian sexual practices, physical characteristics, endurance, contempt of death, hospitality, dress, and passions for gambling and alcohol—before returning to an account of his journey.]

A few miles after leaving the Indian territory, we stopped at the hotel of Mrs. Lucas to dine. She has been a good-looking woman, but now is fatter at her age (only thirty-five) than any woman I ever saw. She is married for the second time, her first husband having been killed in a conflict with the Indians. She takes the entire management of her house, and from what I saw and heard, manages it admirably. At dinner, she sat at the head of the table, her husband sitting at one side; and the dinner, consisting of chicken-pie, ham, vegetables, pudding, and pie, was so neatly put upon the table, so well cooked, and the dessert, consisting of dried fruits, preserved strawberries and plums, was so excellent, and withal the guests seemed to be made so welcome to every thing that was best, that Mrs. Lucas was, in our eyes, almost as meritorious a person as the old lady at the Bridge Inn, at Ferrybridge in Yorkshire, whose good cheer no Scotsman, travelling between London and Edinburgh, ever omitted, if it was in his power, to enjoy. The preserved plum was in as great perfection here as at Ferrybridge. There was wine on the table, as well as brandy and water; and plenty of time was allowed us to partake of our repast. The whole charge was only three-quarters of a dollar for each person. This certainly was as comfortable a meal as we found anywhere in travelling in the United States. We reached Montgomery, the capital of Alabama, in the evening; but the circuit court being here, it was very difficult to find accommodation at either of the hotels.

[Stuart was incorrect. At the time of his visit, Tuscaloosa was the state's capital. It had moved from Cahaba in 1826, and would not be moved to Montgomery until 1847.]

8

Anne Royall
1830
֎

AT FIFTY-FOUR, THE NEWLY-WIDOWED ANNE NEWPORT ROYALL (1769-
1854) FOUND HERSELF DESTITUTE AND TURNED TO PUBLISHING AC-
COUNTS OF HER TRAVELS ACROSS THE UNITED STATES. BETWEEN 1826
AND 1831 SHE PUBLISHED TEN SUCH ACCOUNTS. SHE WAS HIGHLY OPIN-
IONATED: PRO-MASON, SUNDAY MAIL TRANSPORTATION, SOUND MONEY,
TOLERANCE FOR ROMAN CATHOLICS, TERRITORIAL EXPANSION, INTERNAL
IMPROVEMENTS, LIBERAL APPROPRIATIONS FOR SCIENTIFIC RESEARCH AND
STATES RIGHTS REGARDING SLAVERY, AND SHE WAS ANTI-EVANGELICAL,
NULLIFICATION, AND CHURCH-STATE UNION. IN 1829, HER OPPOSITION TO
PRESBYTERIANS RESULTED IN HER CONVICTION IN WASHINGTON AS A
COMMON SCOLD. SHE WAS FAMOUS THROUGHOUT THE COUNTRY, AND HAD
BOTH STRONG FRIENDS AND ENEMIES. HER RELIABLE, BUT HIGHLY PER-
SONAL, UNGRAMMATICAL, AND CANDID PORTRAITS COVERED ALMOST ALL
AMERICAN TOWNS AND NEARLY TWO THOUSAND OF HER FELLOW CITI-
ZENS.

Anne Royall. *Mrs. Royall's Southern Tour, or Second Series
of the Black Book*. 3 vols. Washington: 1831. Volume II, pages
141-148, 179-180.

The Chattehoochie is navigable from this place [Columbus] to
Apalachicola, 300 miles for steam-boats, nine months in the year,
and for small boats all the year.

Toward evening, I set off with Mr. Van Ness, for Fort Mitchell,
and crossing the river in a ferry-boat, we reached the Fort, which

is about six miles distant, with but one accident, and this would have been a serious one if a gentleman had not happened to pass by our carriage, stuck fast in the mud, and neither the horse, though a stout one, nor Mr. V. could move the wheels, and there we were under a delightful shade, formed by a lofty grove, until as luck would have it, a gentleman happened to pass by, and helped us out. The land being a soft rich mould, the least rain, formes it into a quagmire. When we arrived at

FORT MITCHELL,

I desired to know of Mr. V. if there was a tavern, not wishing to intrude upon the officers, whose hospitality I intended neither to court nor refuse. There was, luckily a tavern, and a most delightful, cool, roomy house, with several pleasant cottages in the rear, completely shaded with trees. But not one soul, or body was in the tavern. Mr. Van, having made this discovery, supposing they could not be far off, the door being open, took me from the carriage, and never in my life did I partake of a greater intellectual treat. It fairly restored me to youth, it was so consonant to my feelings and taste—a large, long, cool Piazza, large empty cool rooms, (I hate furniture) an extensive smooth trodden yard, shaded with trees, long seats to sit on. I ranged the premises over in a trice and devoured every thing I met, with heartfelt pleasure. It was a real paradise. After running about till I was weary inhaling the balmy sweets, from the air-wafted fragrance, I sat down and devoured the more distant beauties of this matchless country. This, like Fort Hawkins, is seated on a rise, commanding a view of the handsomest country I had seen yet, all cleared, and in cultivation, like a garden. I do not blame our people for wishing to purchase it, and if they will give me one of those enchanting little spots, I will help them all I can. Indeed it is absurd, to let these Indians lie about here and do nothing—since all the land we own came by the Indians, and through us has been reclaimed from a wilderness! Why not give them back some of our lands on our eastern coast, since they will not work—barren land will do them as well as any.—Let them take, for instance, some of our old fields in Virginia, and rove about there like they do here, and we will feed them—send them corn and meat round by water, and let our citizens who are there, and willing to work, come here—I cannot see why they should object to this. I should not like to send them West, as it would be too far to send them provision, for they are evidently half famished in this fertile spot.

Meantime, I was amused with some carpenters busily at work, furnishing an additional room to the tavern. It appears these workmen were Israelites, and had kept Saturday. Oh! if Dr. Ely only had the power, how he would roast them. This seemed to be the land of liberty—nor did I perceive the strokes of the hammer hurt any one, not even the little ducks which covered the yard, nor a single bee, or butterfly.

After a while Mr. Van Ness found a little boy, whom he assisted in unharnessing the horse, from the gig, and the boy took the horse to the stable.

Soon after this, the landlord came and apologised for being absent, he showed me into one of those little huts, adjoining the tavern, and by this time, his servant women, who had been on a visit, having returned (they were both Indians) he sent them to wait on me, and furnished me with whatever I wanted, one was the cook and one a chambermaid. The hut had two good beds in it, a table and a few chairs. I directed the chambermaid, a very kind, lusty woman, to have tea brought in, and furnish me with pen and ink, paper and a candle, all of which she attended to very promptly. She spoke very good English, and was remarkably well skilled in her business. The name of the landlord, is Johnston, if I remember, a good looking man enough, he had no wife, unless these women were his wives. There were several pretty little children playing about the yard, which these women said were theirs, but they were two handsome to be his.

Meantime, I despatched a note to Maj. Wager, the commandant of the Fort, to apprise him of my arrival. I had passed the Fort, which is some distance from the tavern as I came on, and supposing the officers not aware of my coming in that manner, was ignorant of my presence, I wished them to know it as early as possible, that arrangements might be made, for my visit to inspect the Fort, before the stage called in the morning. One of the Messrs. Crowells, the agent, was then in Washington, the other was at the Fort, that is, he was in a splendid palace, nearly a quarter of a mile distant, though in sight. I did not send to him as it was his place to call on me.

After some time, some stripling, fopish Lieutenants came from the Fort. They were vain, empty, dissipated looking young men, and I tremble for Fort Mitchell. I asked "where the Major was," "he was not at home," but they expected him shortly! Where ought a commandant to be? I had ordered out some chairs for the officers, and one or two decent men, who had called, as I was sitting in the yard before my door, when they came.

While chatting with one or the other of them, expecting the commandant every minute, one of the Lieut's. being rather tipsey, burst out into a titter. I appealed to the rest of the company to send him off, that I was not disposed to suffer such indignities—that I made it a rule, who ever called on me, must treat me with respect. This was a new regulation at F.M. They stared at each other in astonishment, but while I was speaking, a pistol was fired off close by me, and the young man loosing all government of himself, said something impertinent: I therefore excused myself to the company, withdrew into the house and shut the door, leaving them in the yard. I then sent for the landlord and desired him not to suffer any one to intrude upon me, and should the Major come, to show him in. After a while one or two of them came to apologise, but I could see through this, and gave them no countenance, and they walked out.

It was now dark, and the candle was lit, when the landlord came in and a short, broad-faced man with him, which he introduced as Major Wager. The Maj. was quite cool and took a seat in the farther corner of the room, as far from the candle as possible to conceal his broad red face. I soon perceived what he was, and observed, "I thought he was rather slow in paying his respects, that I had a letter for him, but from his conduct, and that of his officers, I did not think him worthy to receive it, and should not deliver it." I complained to him of the outrage of firing the pistol, (evidently done by the drunken Lieut's. to alarm me for their sport.) "But sir you don't frighten me with great guns, much less pistols, you have not a missionary to deal with I assure you, [Mrs. Royall notes that, They had frightened all the Missionaries away.] and I shall call you to an account for the insolence of your Lieut's. A pretty set of fellows you are indeed, placed here to protect people from the Indians, and the Indians could do no more! What are you paid for sir, to eat and get drunk? I shall report you for this." If the fellow had not been a simpleton, he would have sent me a guard from the Fort for the night. He went off muttering, and that was the first and the last I saw of him. I never went near the Fort, nor was I invited [so it appears from this and the conduct of the army at St. Louis, our army is becoming not only useless but danger-ous.] Had he been a gentleman, he would have apologised for the insolence of his men, but there was too much tow there.

Not long after he left me, however, the poor Lieutenant came to my door in tears, and apologized, and I forgave him: he was from Maryland. He said he knew I had it in my power to ruin him, and he would rather blow his brains out, than appear in my book, as he knew he deserved.

There had been a great deal of loud talking, and quite too much noise, for some time, about the tavern, and as it was growing late, I would have retired to bed,—but for the noise I sat up, thinking, they would soon retire, but they grew worse, and finally raised the Indian *war-hoop*, which was evidently like the firing of the pistol, done to frighten me; this pretty treatment to travellers, to an aged, unprotected woman; our government has come to a fine pass in-deed.—The Indians were not half so bad. If Gen. Jackson does not break up this military den of topers, I shall say he is not the man I take him to be—the insult was indeed offered to him, knowing I was his friend. I inquired of the Indian women, if there was an Indian dwelling any where near. They told me there was one within half a mile, and upon the promise of a trifle, she agreed to show me the way. All this being settled, I sent for the landlord, whom I suspected for taking a part in this annoyance. "Now, sir," said I, "if I hear another loud word after this, I quit the place, and seek a place to sleep amongst the Indians in the neighborhood. I am not afraid of your yelling nor shooting; but, sir, I will not be insulted." He was not a bad looking man, yet I am certain, he was concerned in the whole of it, from his awkward excuses about the firing of the pistol, said, "it went off by accident." I presume they make a practice of playing pranks upon all travellers, and thought they would have rare sport with me—like all other knaves however, they missed it widely. I had my bonnet on, and already standing up for a march—"you will say, sir, whether I am to quit the place or not." He promised fair, I lay down and heard no more that night, neither of my two doors having either latch or bolt! This was courage—the place full of Indians, and worse men. Next morning, Maj. Crowell actually condescended to call—probably he had heard something, which rather inclined him to come. But if ever a poor fellow was frightened the landlord was, when he saw me laying the law to Crowell. He repented sorely, when he found whom he had to deal with. If I did not scorch Crowell, I never scorched any one.

A large store here too, the property of Maj. Crowell, to speculate on the Indians. These Crowells are in clover, and could not afford comfort and protection—and comfort with 250 men, (the garrison) at their service, one night to a woman. No wonder Col. Brearly struggled hard to hold his post.—By the way, I saw a son-in-law of the Colonel's here: the meanest man of the whole.

This is the first place I ever was in, where I could say, I had no friend. For the honor of our government, and the U. States' army!—A parcel of paltroons, I could have taken the Fort myself, as I am certain there was not a brave man in it. I had seen Maj. Crowell at Washington city, and he knew enough of me, to have paid more attention.

He plead for forgiveness, and of course he could do no more, and we all took a walk, to look at a large vineyard he is cultivating here—it is very promising indeed. He has several acres in the vine, and I have no doubt, but he will succeed: I think it was the second year, and the vines were very flourishing. The vineyard was near the Major's house, or agent's house, which ever it was one of the

most splendid buildings I have seen in my tour. He invited me to
walk to it and set a while. Not I, indeed, though I am disposed to
overlook the contempt he treated me with, by not paying attention
sooner, I had too much respect for myself to enter his house. We
walked all round the premises, and near the Fort, which no per-
suasion could induce me to enter. Finally we began to understand
each other better—he deeply repented before we parted—as I do
not bear malice, I promised to let them off as easy as possible, (not
the army mind ye) but the Maj. and the landlord, not to conceal the
truth, and I am very sure they will act better for the time to come,
since I have passed my word for them. Mr. Van Ness very politely
waited, till he saw me off in the stage, and though, I am under
particular obligations to him, I was surprised he did not interfere
the preceding night; but as a gentleman remarked once on a like
occasion, perhaps he thought they were in better hands, meaning
myself.

I met with Messrs. Brooke and Simmons here, quite genteel
men, I think the former is of the army, and the latter a Dr.

About nine o'clock, the stage arrived with the same drunken
sot in, who was now to be my companion, quite through the Creek
Nation, to go 100 miles; there was another fellow in, a stage driver,
whom we took in at Knoxville. I was partial to neither; but Mr.
Matthews, though very delicate, was a genteel, amiable man, and
between him, the driver, and myself, we could be a match for the
other two. I was soon assured of this, after conversing with the
driver.

I quit Knox' line at Fort Mitchell and took Capt. Walker's line,
which goes from hence to Mobile. The Captain, it appeared, had
apprised his drivers of my intended tour through the Indian nation, and had given them particular orders respecting me, when I
entered the line—"I know you, said the driver, Capt. Walker told
us all, we must pay strict attention to you." This was enough, they
all heard it, and off we went, through the handsomest country,
doubtless in North America. As for the site of Fort Mitchell, it
must be unrivalled in beauty by any situation on the face of the
earth, in the absence of water scenery.

ROAD TO MONTGOMERY.

As the soil and productions had been continually changing, of course I entered upon a new region of flowers, as I soon perceived, for the whole southern country is one garden of flowers. The flowers in the Creek nation, grow close to the ground; they are a species of pink, of bright scarled red, precisely like the garden pink, and so thick on the ground, that it appears to be covered with red satin. These are again over-topped with white, purple, and blue flowers, none of which I had ever seen before. These were on the dry or upland, and fairly illuminated the woods.

In the moist places, and along the streams, we have the *woodbine*, it runs amongst the underwood, something like the jessamine, and produces a most brilliant flower: also the queen of the forest, the magnolia,—it grows here to a great height, equal to the tallest tree, but was not in bloom; all these, with the same cluster of roses, honey-suckles, bay-trees, &c. &c. described so often, made part of our scenery to-day; but the pink out-shone the whole, as it was more abundant. The land, after leaving Fort Mitchell, soon becomes hilly and thin; on the rivers it is level, and very rich.

The whole way was strewn with Indian camps, but we saw few Indians. They live on the rivers in the summer and attend to their farms, and in fall and winter live in camps on the road side, to sell their productions to travellers, such as corn and fodder for feeding horses. I saw several at Fort Mitchell very handsome, most of them stout men, and their limbs are symmetry itself. No sculptor can shape the human leg so handsome. They must certainly have been designed to be the first of mankind though they are now without energy, that is nine tenths of them. Hot as the weather was they were wrapped in blankets, and seem to care about nothing but red handkerchiefs and beads and red feathers, some of them have fine farms here and there and raise a great many cattle, which winter mostly out on the cane, which abounds on the rivers.

But the whole country is a waste, scarcely a house is seen, and the road badly cut up. I think Maj. W. might bring his men and mend this road, that the mail might go on faster—it would discipline his men full as well as drinking.

We had a poor chance for dinner, I was told, and my kind land-lord, Mr. Dillon, of Columbus, had sent me a most delicious peach pie. I had also drew a considerable ration of dried venison and bread, at Fort Mitchell. Mr. Matthews and I, therefore, fared pretty well. I offered the other two a part [sic.] the stage driver, (who was a sensible, handsome, but dissipated man,) took some, but the other had swallowed the word ruffian too often to swallow my victuals. He had some resentment.

At length we stopped at the only house where dinner was likely to be had, and, as we had to stop here to change horses, I con-cluded to go in and rest on a bed, if there was one, when lo!—dinner was set. Though I had heard an unfavorable account of the lady, for shame sake I sat down with one McBride, who had fallen in with us upon the road, and dined. The rest refused, excepting Mr. Matthews. He was the Sheriff of this region. Ordained by what power I know not, we had fallen in with him some time, and he, keeping up with the stage, amused us with the history of the lady and her husband, though they were never married. They would both get drunk and fight, and she had given him a severe beating quite recently. *Her* eye was black then. He was jealous of her and she was jealous of him, and so it appears they were equally matched. They had parted several times and come together again. She looked like a rattlesnake and he like a copperhead. They had a little child—I pitied it.

Our road was much the same, sometimes rich and sometimes poor, now and then a stream, sometimes we met lots of Indians, men, women and children, all travel together in families. They all have faces alike; the women are very modest—most of them seemed shy of Mr. McBride. Mac had been amongst them often with precepts. He was a good looking young man, but took a few of the drops rather often.

Towards evening we reached

FORT BAINBRIDGE,

where we spent the night. I did not see the Fort, but the house we stopped at was a large elegant tavern and well kept by a Mr. Harris—his wife was a beautiful and pleasant woman, and her neice, Mrs. Eliza Bird, (the wife of Dr. Bird,) who was there on a visit, was the most beautiful creature I ever saw in human form. She was uncommonly tall and majestic and exquisitely shaped, with a fair oval face, and the loveliest eye in human head—and a most bewitching countenance and manners, and her voice is music. She is a perfect curiosity, and approaches nearer perfection than any human being—she is kindness, meekness, and humanity at once. The man whose wife she was, (I did not see him) is certainly most enviable.

We found a great deal of company in the tavern when we came, and the returning stage came in with a great many passengers, of course the servants were thronged, and as I never go to the public table Mrs. Bird sent her own servant to wait on me, and she herself so contrived it that I had a cup of coffee before I set out, which was about one o'clock, A.M.

The passengers in the other stage were merchants going to the North, some of them were known to Mr. Matthews. He observed to them I was alone and would introduce them if they chose. They rather objected, awaiting to see me by stealth when I came to supper, but they were sadly disappointed; meantime I kept close in my room, determined not to gratify them unless they sought my acquaintance like gentlemen, which they did not.

The land was very even here, and a fine garden and farm was attached to the tavern, which is the most delectable treat in the Indian nation. Mr. M. left his horse here and took the stage.

I had nearly forgotten we passed the place where the Georgians and the Indians fought a hard battle in the night, and the Indians boasted they would have whipped the former if it had not been for the approach of day light. I also saw another den of infamous U. S. soldiers, on the way. We breakfasted at the house of Capt. Walker which is inside of a fort, I forget the name. But I was sorry not to find the Captain at home. He keeps a good house and attentive servants.

This day's journey was much like the preceding, excepting the Pinks which had changed to blue; but after we crossed Line Creek, which divides Alabama from the Creek nation, the land then is very rich, with vast plantations of corn, cotton, and sugar. We passed Mount M'Gee [Mt. Meigs], after crossing Line Creek; a beautiful situation, with a post office, tavern, store, blacksmith shop, and two or three good houses. It is handsomely shaded by china trees. We also passed, in the Indian nation, the deserted house and farm of *Sukey Randall*, a black woman, who was rich, married to a white man, and her children all married white people. She has removed to Arkansas.

On the bank of Line Creek I saw the grave of the celebrated and lamented Riley. We arrived at

MONTGOMERY

Sometime before night, having crossed big Uchee, little Uchee, Persimon's Creek, Cubahatchees, another stream, besides Line Creek, all handsome streams.

At Montgomery, I parted with Mr. Matthews, a most amiable man, to whose politeness I am much indebted. He lived a few miles distant, at Washington, a town on Alabama river.

9

Thomas Hamilton
April 1831

⚜

F OLLOWING THREE YEARS AT GLASGOW UNIVERSITY, THOMAS HAMILTON (1789-1842) OBTAINED AN ARMY COMMISSION IN 1810. CAPTAIN HAMILTON WAS SERIOUSLY WOUNDED IN THE PENINSULA CAMPAIGN; HE SUBSEQUENTLY SERVED IN NOVA SCOTIA AND NEW BRUNSWICK AND WITH THE ARMY OF OCCUPATION IN FRANCE. AFTER RETIRING AT HALF PAY IN 1818, HE RETURNED TO HIS NATIVE SCOTLAND WHERE HE TOOK UP WRITING. SOME READERS SEE HAMILTON AS FLIPPANT AND HAUGHTY, AND OTHERS SEE HIM AS OBJECTIVE AND UNPREJUDICED. NEVERTHELESS, HIS SOMETIMES EXAGGERATED AND HUMOROUS ACCOUNT OF HIS AMERICAN TRAVELS WAS SO POPULAR THAT WITHIN A DECADE IT HAD BEEN TRANSLATED INTO FRENCH AND GERMAN.

Thomas Hamilton. *Men and Manners in America*. Philadelphia: Cary, Lea and Blanchard, 1833. Volume II, pages 335-344.

At four o'clock P. M., we started in the mail stage for Fort Mitchell. There were unfavourable reports abroad of the state of the rivers, which were asserted to be impassable; but I had so often experienced that difficulties, formidable at a distance, become insignificant on nearer approach, that I determined to push on at all hazards. In the present case, my determination was unlucky, for it involved both my companion and myself in some little danger, and occasioned considerable detention.

We accomplished the first stage without difficulty of any kind, but with the second commenced the tug of war. Our first obstacle was a bayou of such depth, that in crossing it, the water was ankle-deep in the bottom of the carriage. Night had set in before we reached Lime [Line] Creek, which, though generally a slow and sluggish stream, was now swelled into a very formidable torrent. It requires experience to understand the full danger of crossing such a river, and, perhaps, fortunately, I did not possess it. But both the passengers and coachman were under considerable alarm, and one of the former, a Louisianian planter, in broken English threatened the black ferryman with instant death in case of negligence or blunder. This caused some merriment; but Sambo, who was evidently under no alarm, took the matter very coolly. The coach was run into the ferry-boat, and by means of a hawser stretched across the river, we soon found ourselves in safety on the opposite bank.

We were now in the territory of the Creek Indians, and in consequence of the darkness, it was soon found impossible to proceed without torches. We tried in vain to procure them at several of the Indian encampments, but were at last fortunate enough to discover an axe in the coach, with which abundance were soon cut from the neighbouring pines. I have had occasion to say a great deal about roads in these volumes, but I pronounce that along which our route lay on the present occasion, to be positively, comparatively, and superlatively, the *very worst* I have ever travelled in the whole course of my peregrinations. The ruts were axle-deep, and huge crevices occasionally occurred, in which, but for great strategy on the part of the coachman, the vehicle must have been engulfed.

In such circumstances none of the passengers seemed ambitious of the dangerous distinction of keeping his seat. We all walked, each armed with a pine torch, and the party, to a spectator, must have had very much the aspect of a funeral procession. Nothing, however, could be more beautiful than the scene presented by the forest. The glare of our torches, as we continued slowly advancing amid the darkness; the fires of the Indian encampments seen at a distance through the trees, and the wild figures by which they were surrounded; the multitude of fire-flies which flickered every where among the foliage,—formed a combination of objects which more than compensated in picturesque beauty, for all the difficulties we had yet encountered.

We had to pass two swamps on a sort of pavement formed of logs of trees, or what is called in America, a "corduroy road." The operation, though one of some difficulty, was effected without accident. The country, as we advanced, presented greater inequalities of surface. Stumps of trees often came in contact with the wheels, and brought the whole machine to a stand-still; trees which had been blown over by the wind sometimes lay directly across the road, and it was with difficulty that the united exertions of the passengers succeeded in removing them.

In spite of all obstacles, however, we reached an Indian tavern, where we changed horses and had supper. We were now beyond the region of bread, and our fare consisted of eggs, broiled venison, and cakes of Indian corn fried in some kind of oleaginous matter. The venison was tolerable, and the biscuits of my friend, the Mobile baker, I bade defiance to fate in the way of eating.

On returning to the coach, we found the night had become one of rain. The clouds began discharging their contents in no very alarming profusion, but this soon changed, and the rain absolutely descended in torrents. The pine torches refused to burn; the wind roared loudly among the trees; streams came rushing down the gulleys, and inundated the road, and in spite of greatcoats and waterproof cloaks, in less than an hour I found myself fairly drenched to the skin.

At length the horses, on getting half way up a hill, became fairly exhausted, and no application of the lash could induce them to proceed. The passengers all pushed most lustily, but the horses were obstinate, and gave us no assistance. In short, we were evidently hard and fast for the night, and resigning all hope of immediate extrication, the driver was despatched on one of the leaders to the next stage for assistance, while in doleful mood, and absolutely saturated with water, we reseated ourselves in the coach to await his reappearance.

It would not, in truth, be easy to conceive a set of men in more miserable pickle. The storm, instead of abating, continued to increase. The peals of thunder were tremendous. The lightning split a huge pine-tree within a few yards of us, and one of the passengers declared he was struck blind, and did not recover his sight for an hour or two. The rain beat in through the sides and covering of the carriage, as if in wantonness of triumph to drench men who, sooth to say, were quite wet enough already. In short,

> "Such sheets of fire, such bursts of horrid thunder,
> Such groans of roaring wind and rain, I never
> Remember to have heard."

From one o'clock in the morning until seven did we continue in this comfortless condition, when we were somewhat cheered by the appearance of the driver, who, we afterwards discovered, had been sleeping very comfortably in an Indian cottage in the neighborhood. He brought with him a couple of Negroes, but no additional horses, and of course it was quite preposterous to suppose that the poor animals, which had been standing all night without food, and exposed to the storm, could now perform a task to which they had formerly proved unequal. The attempt was made, however; and to lighten the coach, our baggage was tossed out upon the road. Neither the Negroes, horses, nor passengers, could move the coach one inch from its position. There it was, and there it was destined to remain. Our last hope of extrication had now failed us, and it became necessary to find shelter and hospitality as best we could.

Luckily an Indian cottage was discovered at no great distance, where, by the help of a blazing fire, we succeeded in drying our drenched garments. In the course of the day a bullock wagon was despatched for the mail-bags and luggage, and there was evidently nothing for it but roughing it with a good grace.

On the part of those on whose privacy we had intruded, our welcome was tranquil, but apparently sincere. Our host—one of the handsomest Indians I have ever seen—spread before us his whole store of eggs, venison, and Indian corn, with the air of a forest gentleman. His two wives, with greater advantages of toilet, would probably have been good-looking, but being unfortunately rather dirty, and clad only in a blanket and blue petticoat, the sum of their attractions was by no means overpowering. The children were nearly naked, yet graceful in all their motions. Their chief amusement seemed to consist in the exercise of the crossbow.

One of the passengers produced a musical snuff-box, which occasioned great excitement in the women and children. The men were too dignified or phlegmatic to betray either pleasure or astonishment. Our host, however, was evidently delighted with an air-gun with which several birds were killed for his amusement. He then asked permission to take a shot, and hit a dollar with great accuracy at about thirty yards.

It somewhat lowered the ideas of romance connected with these Indians, to find that they are, many of them, slave-owners. But slavery among this simple people assumes a very different aspect from any under which I had yet beheld it. The negroes speak English, and generally act as *dragomen* in any intercourse with the whites. They struck me as being far handsomer than any I had yet seen, partly, perhaps, from being unhabituated to severe labour, and partly from some slight admixture of Indian blood. I conversed with several who described their bondage as light, and spoke of their master and his family with affection.

To the lash they are altogether unaccustomed, and when married, live in houses of their own, round which they cultivate a patch of ground. The negro and Indian children are brought up together on a footing of perfect equality, and the government of the family seemed entirely patriarchal.

The weather had become fine, and the day passed more pleasantly than the night. The Indian territory being beyond the reach of American law, is sought as a place of refuge by criminals, and those to whom the restraints of civilized society are habitually irksome. These men intermarry with the natives, among whom they contribute to spread guilt and demoralization. In truth, the majority are ruffians, whose proneness to crime is here alike unchecked by principle, religion, public opinion, or dread of punishment.

Towards evening, two of this class came in, and chose to pass the night in drinking. Nothing more offensive than their manners and conversation can readily be conceived. After bearing patiently with this annoyance for an hour or two, it at length became intolerable, and, in order to escape, I spread my cloak in a corner of the cabin and endeavoured to sleep. But this was impossible. The noise, the demands for liquor, the blasphemy, the wrangling, were unceasing. At length, one of the men drew his dirk, and attempted to assassinate his opponent, who succeeded, however, in seizing him by the throat, and both rolled upon the floor. I immediately jumped up, and the alarm roused our host, who, with the assistance of a slave, barely succeeded in saving the life of one of the combatants. He was at first insensible. His mouth was wide open; his face and lips were livid; his eyes seemed bursting from their sockets, and, on being raised, his head hung down upon his shoulder. His lungs, however, made a convulsive effort to regain their action. There was a loud and sudden gurgle, and he became better. The other man was prevailed on to depart; and towards four in the morning, silence, broken only by the snoring of some of its inmates, reigned in the cottage.

Sleep, however, was impossible, under the incessant attacks of a multitude of blood-suckers, which, flea for man, would have outnumbered the army of Xerxes. But morning came, and fortunately with it, a coach intended to convey us on our journey. Our host could not be prevailed on to make any charge for our entertainment, but one of his wives received all we chose to offer, and appeared satisfied with its amount. Not an article of the baggage was found missing, and, on departing, I shook hands with the whole establishment—Negroes included—to the great scandal of the American passengers.

Even by daylight our way was beset by difficulties. First came Kilbeedy Creek, which we crossed by as awkward and rickety a bridge as can well be imagined. Then came Pessimmon's swamp, which presented a delightful corduroy road, some parts of which had been entirely absorbed by the morass. At length, we reached the inn kept by an American polygamist, with three Indian wives. The breakfast was no better than might be expected in such an establishment. It consisted of bad coffee, rancid venison, and corn cakes, no eggs, no milk, no butter. Our host, apparently, had no great taste in regard to wives. One was round as a hogshead; another skin and bone; of the third I saw, or at least remember, nothing.

The meal concluded, we again set forward. Our route lay through one continued pine forest. In the course of the day we passed many Indian wigwams, and a few houses of a better order, surrounded by small enclosures. The road by no means improved, and, in order to relieve the horses, we were compelled to walk. At one place it was completely obstructed by a huge fallen tree, which delayed our progress for at least two hours. About three o'clock we dined at the house of a half-caste Indian, on the usual fare, venison and Indian corn.

In the course of the evening we passed several heights which afforded extensive, if not fine, views of the neighbouring country. The road, too, became somewhat better, and, being composed of sand without stones, though heavy for the horses, was not uncomfortable, for the passengers. For myself, I never experienced greater fatigue. During the two preceding nights, I had never closed an eye, and when, at four in the morning, we reached a small tavern, where—owing to the desertion of the moon—it was found necessary to wait till daylight, I cast myself on the floor, and in a moment was asleep.

Daylight soon came, and I was again roused from my slumbers. We were yet fourteen miles from Fort Mitchell, and for the greater part of the distance, were compelled to make progress on foot. The sun rose beautifully above the dark tops of the pine trees, but he was never gazed on by more languid eyes. At ten o'clock we reached Fort Mitchell, having in twenty-four hours accomplished a distance of only ninety miles.

Fort Mitchell is garrisoned by a detachment of the United States army, in order to prevent aggressions on the Georgian frontier by the Indians. Beyond the limits of the fort there are,—if I remember rightly,—only three houses, one of which is a tavern. Its accommodations were far from comfortable, but the landlord was civil, and evidently disposed to do his best in our behalf. Under such circumstances we made no complaint, though—judging from the scantiness of our meals—his larder must have rivalled in opulence the shop of the apothecary in Romeo and Juliet.

My first effort was to procure a place in the coach to Augusta, but in this I was disappointed. Fort Mitchell seemed a sort of *trou de rat* which it was difficult to get into, and still more difficult to get out of. I was detained there for nearly a week, and never did time pass more slowly. Had my sojourn been voluntary, I should probably have found a great deal to interest and amuse, but an enforced residence is never pleasant, and, but for the privilege of grumbling, would be intolerable.

The officers of the garrison lived in the hotel, and took pleasure in showing kindness to a stranger. I rode with them through the neighbouring forest, and was indebted to them for much valuable information relative to the Indians. During my stay, there was a Ball Play, in which two neighbouring tribes contended for superiority. One of these was the Creeks, the other the Ewitches, a very small tribe which occupy a district in the Creek territory, and still retain all their peculiarities of language and custom.

On the appointed morning we repaired to the scene of action, where a considerable number of spectators—chiefly Indians—had already assembled. The players on each side soon appeared, and retired to the neighbouring thickets to adjust their toilet for the game. While thus engaged, either party endeavoured to daunt their opponents by loud and discordant cries. At length they emerged with their bodies entirely naked except the waist, which was encircled by a girdle. Their skin was besmeared with oil, and painted fantastically with different colours. Some wore tails, others necklaces made of the teeth of animals, and the object evidently was to look as ferocious as possible.

After a good deal of preliminary ceremony, the game began. The object of either party was to send the ball as far as possible into their adversary's ground, and then to make it pass between two poles, erected for the purpose of demarcation. I certainly never saw a finer display of agile movement. In figure the Creek Indians are tall and graceful. There is less volume of muscle than in Englishmen, but more activity and freedom of motion. Many of the players were handsome men, and one in particular might have stood as the model of an Apollo. His form and motions displayed more of the *idéal* than I had ever seen actually realized in a human figure. The Ewitches were by no means so good-looking as their competitors.

The game is accompanied with some danger, both to those engaged in it and to the spectators. It is quite necessary for the latter to keep clear of the *mélée*, for in following the ball, the whole body of the players sweep on like a hurricane, and a gouty or pursy gentleman could be safe only when perched on the boughs of a tree. At length the Creeks were victorious, and the air rang with savage shouts of triumph. The poor Ewitches, chop-fallen, quitted the field, declaring, however, that none but their worst players had taken part in the game. The victors danced about in all the madness of inordinate elation, and the evening terminated in a profuse jollification, to which I had the honour of contributing.

During my stay at Fort Mitchell I saw a good deal of the United States troops. The discipline is very lax, and being always separated in small detachments, they have no opportunity of being exercised in field movements. On Sunday there was a dress parade, which I attended. Little was done, but that little in the most slovenly manner. It is only justice to the officers to state, that they are quite aware of the deficiencies of the service to which they belong. "You will laugh," they said, "at our want of method and discipline, but the fault is not ours; we cannot help it. The service is unpopular, we receive no support from the government, and we have no means of maintaining proper subordination." A non-commissioned officer, who had formerly been in our [British] service, and, therefore, understood what soldiers should be, in answering some questions, treated the whole affair as a joke. He entered the American service, he said, because there was easy work, and little trouble of any sort. He had no intention of remaining long in it, for he could do better in other ways. There was no steady and effective command kept over the soldiers, and yet there was a great deal of punishment. Even from the small detachment at Fort

Mitchell desertions happened every week. Whenever a man became tired of his duty, off he went, bag and baggage, and pursuit was hopeless.

The truth is, that men accustomed to democracy can never be brought to submit patiently to the rigours of military discipline. The nation take pride in their navy, but none in their army. The latter service is neglected; there is no encouragement for the display of zeal in the officers, and the stations are so remote as to remove the troops entirely from public observation. The people care nothing for a set of invisible beings mewed up in some petty forts on the vast frontier, who have no enemy to contend with, and are required to brave nothing but fever and moschetoes. Then, when a case connected with the enforcement of discipline comes before the civil courts, the whole feeling is in favour of the prosecutor. I remember a curious instance of this, which was related to me by an officer of distinction in the United Service [sic.] army. A soldier found guilty, by a court-martial, of repeated desertions, was sentenced to a certain period of imprisonment, and loss of pay. The man underwent the allotted punishment, and on being liberated, immediately brought actions against all the members of the court-martial. The ground taken up was this:—The articles of war state, that whoever is guilty of desertion, shall "suffer death, or such other punishment as, by a general court-martial, shall be awarded." It was maintained, that, by this clause, the court were empowered to inflict only one punishment, and that, in passing sentence of imprisonment and stoppage of pay, they had inflicted two. The jury gave a verdict and high damages against the members of the court, who received no assistance nor protection of any kind from the government.

On leaving Fort Mitchell, we crossed the Chatahouchy (a very considerable river, of which I had never heard,) and entered the State of Georgia.

10

Sol Smith
May 1832

❦

SOLOMON FRANKLIN SMITH (1801-1869) WAS FIRST ATTRACTED TO THE THEATER IN ALBANY, NEW YORK, WHERE, AT SIXTEEN, HE AT-TEMPTED TO RUN AWAY WITH A THEATRICAL TROUPE. AFTER MORE THAN A DECADE OF JOURNALISTIC WORK AND WORK WITH TRAVELING THEATRICAL TROUPES, IN 1827 HE BECAME A FULL-TIME ACTOR AND THEATRICAL MAN-AGER. BY 1835 HE WAS A STAR PLAYING IN ST. LOUIS, NEW YORK AND PHILADELPHIA. THAT YEAR HE JOINED NOAH LUDLOW IN MOBILE; LUDLOW AND SMITH BECAME ONE OF THE MOST IMPORTANT THEATRICAL COMPANIES IN THE WEST.

IN 1853 SMITH LEFT THE THEATER FOR THE LAW, WHICH HE PRAC-TICED IN ST. LOUIS. IN 1861, AS A MEMBER OF THE MISSOURI STATE CONVENTION, HE HELPED KEEP THAT STATE FROM SECEDING FROM THE UNION.

Solomon Franklin Smith. *Theatrical Management in the West and South for Thirty Years.* New York: Harper and Brothers, 1868. Pages 77-78.

We made another short season in Montgomery, and then, our arrangements for traveling being completed, we wended our way through the Creek nation into Georgia.

ADVENTURE IN THE CREEK NATION.

The company traveled in barouches, and the baggage was sent in a large Pennsylvania road wagon. We passed through the Creek na-

tion about five years previous to the commencement of the distur-
bances which ended in sending the Indians to Arkansas. One afternoon we halted for refreshment at the residence of a chief, where
about one hundred Indians were assembled, drinking and carous-
ing. One of our number, by name John Carter, who had undertaken to perform the duties of general caterer for the party, purchased a gallon of milk, and the usual quantum of sugar and rum,
of which ingredients, with the addition of a little grated nutmeg,
he was busily engaged in forming that delicious mixture well known
by Southern travelers as *milk punch*. Now it happened that John
had been dreading this journey for some months, having taken up
the idea that we should most assuredly be attacked and robbed (if
not murdered) while traveling through this same Creek nation. My
brother and myself formed a plan to have some sport out of his
fears, and proceeded to execute it thus: I went to the chief, and
offered to give a dollar to four Indians who would run a mile, and
"keep up" with the Jersey wagon which I pointed out to him, at the
same time showing him the man who was to drive. The chief immediately agreed to the proposal, and called four young men from
their sports to give them their instructions. While this was going
on, my brother called John mysteriously aside, and asked him what
he had been saying or doing to the Indians. "I have not said a word
to them," replied John, innocently, "except to ask them for these
materials, which they furnished me willingly, and charged a pretty
good price for too. There, taste that, and say if you don't approve
of it: you won't get such a bowl of punch as that again in a hurry,
I can tell you." At this juncture I came up and asked our worthy
caterer the same question previously propounded by my brother,
and added, "The Indians seem to have taken offense at some one
of our party." This caused John to open his eyes a little, and his
looks became somewhat disturbed. "I can't imagine who has been
saying or doing any thing to offend them." "Nor I either," said
John, "unless the tarnal fools have taken offense at my saying that
ninepence a quart was a devilish high price for milk." "That's it,"
replied I, "to a certainty; these natives are very tenacious of their
character, and can not bear to be charged with extortion." Here
John cast some anxious glances toward a group of Indians, who

seemed observing us attentively, and talking aside, every now and then pointing toward John, and then looking at the Jersey wagon which belonged to him and his family. "What do they mean by that, I wonder? They seem to direct their attention entirely to *me* and old *Copp*"—(that was the name of the horse)— "I don't know what to make of it, I'm sure." Thus spoke John, while big drops of sweat began to be apparent on his brow. "I do really begin to think they have some hostile design upon you," said I; "and, now I think of it, I recollect an expression of one of them, just as I passed those fellows with the hatchets, which confirms me in the opinion that they mean something." "What expression—what did the bloody-minded rascals say?" demanded John, in a tremor of apprehension, not a little increased by certain flourishes of hatchets by the savages, and a low murmur which met his ear, and which his fears interpreted into a death-song. "I don't understand the Creek language perfectly," was my reply, "but, from what I could gather, I am disposed to think they are highly offended at something; that tall fellow observed to the others that *ekrecrlculaka-hooch-ichopetehick*—which translated into English, means, *if people don't like the price of milk, they had better not drink it*; to which that fellow who is now looking this way replied, *Chackle-damnationuphillanddowntumbleum—chook!* which, as near as I can make it out, means, *they'll follow you to the Chattahoochie River but they'll have revenge!* By this time John's fears had got the better of his love for punch, and he began to look round for his hat and gloves. Every movement was watched by the four savages, who had their instructions to chase the wagon a mile. "Here— stop a bit—I think, for fear of accidents, I'd better be off. If you'll take care of the ladies and pay for the punch, I'll quietly take old Copp and put." We agreed with him that perhaps it was best, for fear of accidents, that he should effect his escape, as *he* appeared to be the only one of the party the savages had any designs against. So, without even tasting the excellent punch he had brewed, he slipped round the barn and put the bridle on Captain Copp. The four Indians kept him in view all the time, but the fugitive appeared not to notice them. When he had fairly got the reins in his hands and mounted the Jersey, he cast one last look toward us and the bowl of punch, another (of quite a different kind) toward the four hostile savages, and gave the whip to old Copp. The crack of the whip was followed by a short of whoop from the Indians. Off started the Jersey, with John standing up and lashing old Copp at every jump, and off started the four Indians in pursuit. Such a race has seldom been seen in the Creek nation.

Having drunk and settled for the punch, we pursued our journey at leisure, forming various conjectures how far our frightened companion would travel that night. About half a mile from the starting-place we found John's traveling-cap, and began to fear some accident might have befallen its owner; three quarters of a mile farther we found the four Indians dancing in the road, and tossing up in the air something which resembled a *human scalp!* "Heavens and earth!" I exclaimed, "is it possible our foolish joke has ended in the destruction of our poor friend?" On approaching the Indians, our worst fears were removed by one of them throwing us the scalp, which turned out to be John's *scratch*, that valuable article having been lost in the race! We paid the Indians the promised dollar, and, in return, they gave us a parting yell through their fingers which made the pine forest ring again.

About eight miles farther on we found our friend sitting on a log by the road-side, the perspiration bursting from his bald head in drops as large as bullets; Captain Copp was in a complete foam. "Thank God!" exclaimed the poor fellow, as we approached, "you have escaped the blood-thirsty savages. If General Jackson don't take this matter up, he's not the man I take him for, that's all." Having restored John his wig, and removed his fears of immediate danger by telling him we had met the Indians returning from the chase, we began to question him concerning his miraculous escape. "Gentlemen," said he, "it's all owing to that glorious horse, Captain Copp, who is the greatest animal living: it took him to take me through the dangers of this day. The infernal villains poured in upon me from all quarters; there was one behind every tree ready to intercept me; and them their outrageous yells and whooping—they ring in my ears yet. I lost my hat and wig in the strife, for at one time there were about a dozen in the wagon endeavoring to scalp me; but, knocking over five of the foremost of the ruthless

villains, and laying the whip boldly on to old Copp, I managed to
get out of their infernal clutches, and am still alive."

Some days after this adventure, one of our party asked John
how many Indians he thought there were in pursuit of him. "I can
not be certain," replied he; "I had but little time to think of count-
ing them at the time; but, from a calculation I have made since, I
think that, without taking into the account the squaws and papooses,
who are considered non-combatants, there couldn't have been much
less that FIFTEEN HUNDRED."

I could fill volumes with accounts of this and other journeys
through this then uncultivated country; but I spare the reader all
details, and carry him straight through, barely stopping by the way
to say that we "put up" the second night, on this particular occasion, at the BLACK WARRIOR'S, where the warrior's wife (the
warrior himself being off on a hunt) gave us rather "lenten fare,"
but fed our horses well; bad beds, well peopled with fleas and
bed-bugs; and made enormous charges for our accommodation.
At Mr. Elliott's, twelve miles from Columbus, we fared much better, being served with an excellent supper of fish, which the landlord informed me he caught in great abundance—sometimes as
many as 300 a night—in a trap!

Sunday morning, May 20th, 1832, we crossed the Chattahoochie
River, leaving Alabama behind us.

GEORGIA! generous, hospitable Georgia! How well do I remember my sensations when first entering upon your soil! It was
Sunday, and the streets of Columbus were filled with gayly-dressed
citizens and Creek Indians. The arrival of a theatrical company
created a decided sensation.

11

Tyrone Power
December 1834

⚜

WILLIAM GRATTAN TYRONE POWER (1797-1841), A NATIVE OF IRE-
LAND, JOINED THE THEATER AT FOURTEEN, AGAINST HIS MOTHER'S
WISHES. HIS REPUTATION ON THE LONDON STAGE WAS BASED ON PARTS AS
THE COMIC IRISHMAN. HE MADE FOUR AMERICAN TOURS: 1833-35, 1837,
1838, AND 1840. HE PERISHED WHEN THE *PRESIDENT*, THE LARGEST
STEAMSHIP OF THE TIME, WENT DOWN IN STORM AS HE WAS RETURNING TO
ENGLAND. HIS HUMOR, EXPRESSED AS A COMIC ACTOR AND AS THE AU-
THOR OF IRISH FARCES AND A COMEDY, IS READILY EVIDENT IN THE AC-
COUNT WHICH FOLLOWS. HIS STANCE IS POSITIVE; UNLIKE SO MANY FOR-
EIGN TRAVELERS HE SAW AMERICANS AS "CLEAR-HEADED, ENERGETIC,
FRANK, AND HOSPITABLE."

Tyrone Power. *Impressions of America; During the Years
1833, 1834, and 1835*. 2 vols. Philadelphia: Carey, Lea and
Blanchard, 1836. Volume II, pages 86-101.

COLUMBUS.

At the hour of two, A. M. we reached the city of Columbus, on the
Chattahoochee, the river dividing Alabama from Georgia.

Here we halted for a day and a night; and the time I employed,
in company with my two New York fellow-travellers, in paying a
visit to the Choctaw tribe of Indians, who possess a reserve lying
west of the river.

We procured three stout nags, and early in the morning crossed
the very fine bridge which spans this rapid stream close to the

falls. On the Alabama side we found ourselves within a wild-look-
ing village, scattered through the edge of the forest, bearing the
unattractive name of Sodom [Girard; today's Phenix City]; few of
its denizens were yet stirring; they are composed chiefly of "min-
ions o' the moon," outlaws from the neighbouring States. Gam-
blers, and other desperate men, here find security from their numbers, and from the vicinity of a thinly inhabited Indian country,
whose people hold them in terror, yet dare not refuse them a hid-
ing-place. These bold outlaws, I was informed, occasionally assemble to enjoy an evening's frolic in Columbus, on which occasion they cross the dividing bridge in force, all armed to the teeth;
the warrants in the hands of the U.S. Marshal are at such times
necessarily suspended, since to execute a caption would require a
muster greater than any within his command. If unmolested, the
party usually proceed to the nearest hotel, drink deeply, make what
purchases they require for the ladies of their colony, pay promptly,
and, gathering the stragglers together, retire peaceably into the territory, wherein their present rule is by report absolute. The condition of this near community, and the crimes perpetrated by its
members, were alluded to within the town with a mingled senti-
ment of detestation and fear.

A short way within the forest we overtook a man riding a rough
pony, of whom I inquired the best route to be pursued for falling in
with the Indian settlements; the man immediately volunteered to
ride with us for a few hours; adding, that he saw we were strangers
from the North; that he was "a Vermont man himself, and had
nothing particular to do just then."

This was a lucky rencontre: the volunteer guide we had secured appeared perfectly familiar with every turn of the number-
less narrow foot-paths leading from one location to another; and,
under his guidance, we visited several.

The condition of the majority of these poor people seemed
wretched in the extreme: most of the families were living in
wigwams, built of bark or green boughs, of the frailest and least
comfortable construction; not an article of furniture, except a kettle,
was in the possession of this class. A few, however, were here who
had erected log-houses, cleared a little land, and were also in the

possession of a stove or two; we halted at a group of four of these little dwellings, where, under a shed, a fine negro wench was occupied frying bacon and making cakes of wheaten flour for her master's supper, who, she informed us, was absent on a hunting expedition. Within the log-huts sat the squaws of the party, all busily employed sewing beads on moccasins, or ornamenting deerskin pouches, after the fashion of the dames of old in the absence of their true knights; our guide addressed these ladies roughly enough; but without eliciting any reply more encouraging than a sort of "Ugh! ugh!" unaccompanied by a single look. The negro girl, however, had not adopted the taciturnity of the tribe, but readily chatted with us, explaining, amongst other matters, the nature of the contents of the boiler, whose savoury smell greatly attracted our attention. She said it was composed of Indian corn, boiled a great deal and slowly, with only a little salt for seasoning; affirming, that the Indians preferred this simple dish to all other dainties. For myself, I gave a decided vote in favour of the fried rashers, and the nice little cakes baked in the ashes; of these we partook freely, at the solicitation of the good-humoured cook, who, with right Indian hospitality assured us there was plenty more.

Returning, we encountered several members of this tribe who had been passing the day in Columbus; some were on foot, others riding, but all more or less elevated; a few of the women were good-looking, and to their credit, all of them sober.

As we repassed Sodom, the sound of revelry proclaimed the orgies resumed. The rain, which had hitherto held up, once more began to descend with a determination of purpose that boded us no good; we spurred over the covered bridge and were soon after housed again in Georgia.

At our hotel I encountered a gentleman who, a few weeks before, had been a fellow-passenger with me from New York to Charleston; but his advance had been less prosperous that mine: indeed, a brief relation of what he had endured sufficed to reconcile me to any little fatigue that fell to my lot. It appeared that, three weeks previous to this meeting of ours, he had quitted Columbus in a steamer going down to Appalachicola: they had proceeded some three hundred miles on their way, when in the night, the passengers were roused from sleep by the alarm of "fire!" The boat was, in fact, a mass of flame by the time the first persons reached the deck. My informant, with many others, immediately jumped overboard: the steamer was run on the bank; and, with the exception of two persons drowned, the rest of her passengers and crew were landed in the forest; most of them with nothing in the shape of covering excepting their night-clothes. Luckily, there were only two ladies of the party; and their condition may be imagined, living for four days in the forest swamp without any other than temporary huts for shelter, and in all other respects most scantily provided for, as the suddenness of the fire prevented any saving of stores or provisions.

At the end of four days the up-river steamer was hailed on its passing, and, getting on board of this, they were in a few days after landed where I found my informant waiting for the next boat. It appeared that the fire was attributed to a slave who had been the day before flogged for mutiny, and who, according to the evidence of his fellows, had threatened some such revenge.

During the afternoon I walked about this thriving frontier town, despite a smart shower: the stores were well supplied, the warehouses filled with cotton, and in all quarters were groups of the neighbouring planters busied in looking after the sale of their produce, and making such purchases as their families required.

Numerous parties of Indians,—Creeks and Choctaws,— roamed about from place to place, mostly drunk, or seeking to become so as quickly as possible: with each party of the natives I observed a negro-man, the slave of some one present, but commonly well dressed in the European manner, having an air of superior intelligence to his masters, and evidently exercising over them the power and influence derived from superior knowledge: the negroes, in fact, appeared the masters, and the red-men the slaves.

Along the river-front of the town, a situation wildly beautiful, I observed several dwellings of mansion-like proportions, and others of a similar character in progress. I should say, that nowhere in this South country have I yet seen a place which promises more of the prosperity increasing wealth can bestow than this; or one that, from all I learned, is more wanting in all that men usually consider most worth possessing,—personal security, reasonable comfort, and well-executed law. In place of these, affrays ending in blood are said to be frequent, apprehensions few, acquittal next to certain even in the event of trial, and the execution of a white man a thing unknown.

In the midst of all this, be it understood, I do not consider that a traveller runs the least risk; robbery, or murder for the sake of mere plunder, never occurs; and to a stranger the rudest of these frontier spirits are usually exceedingly civil; but idleness, hot blood, and frequent stimulants make gambling or politics ready subjects for quarrels, and, as the parties always go armed, an affray is commonly fatal to some of those concerned.

As the population steadily advances, these wild spirits melt away before it, some becoming good citizens, others clearing out before the onward march of civilization: their sway is therefore yearly decreasing in force within the States, their sphere becoming limited in proportion as persons interested in the support of law increase; already, each season, numbers seek freedom from restraint within the Mexican territory, where an infusion of such blood will be productive of strange events in Texas; and if this fine territory be not, within a very short period, rendered over-hot a berth for its Mexican proprietors, "coming events cast their shadows before" to very little purpose.

TRAVELLING THROUGH THE CREEK-NATION, THE ALABAMA RIVER DOWN TO MOBILE.

A LITTLE before midnight, my two New York *compagnons du voyage* and myself took our seats in the mail for Montgomery, on the Alabama river. We found ourselves the sole occupants of the vehicle, and were congratulating each other on the chance, when we heard directions given to the driver to halt at Sodom, for the purpose of taking up a gentleman and his lady,—*Anglice*, a gambler and his mistress.

It was dark as pitch and raining hard when we set out: a few minutes found us rumbling along the enclosed bridge, amidst the mingled roar of the rain, our wheels, and the neighbouring falls: the flood passing below us had in the course of the last ten hours risen nearly twenty feet; its rush was awful.

At one of the first houses in the redoubtable border village the stage halted, and a couple of trunks were added to our load; next, a female was handed into the coach, followed by her protector. The proportions of neither could at this time be more than guessed at; and not one syllable was exchanged by any of the parties. In a few minutes we were again under weigh, and plunging through the forest.

We reached Fort-Mitchell about daylight, where formerly a considerable garrison was kept up: the post is now, however, abandoned. Here an unanticipated treat awaited us, for we were compelled to leave our, by this time, tolerably warm stage, for one fairly saturated with the rain that had fallen during the night. Our luggage was pitched into the mud by the coachman, who had only one assistant; so we were fain to lend a hand, instead of standing shivering by, until the trunks were fished out, and disposed of on the new stage. A delay here of an hour and a half enabled me, however, to stroll back, and take a look at the deserted barrack. By this time too the day was well out; the sky broke with a more cheerful look than for some days back had favoured us, and was hailed by us all with great pleasure.

I prepared my 'baccy, and climed on to the box by the driver, resolute to hold on there as long as possible. For five hours we got along at the rate of four miles an hour, through a forest of pine growing out of a sandy soil, without any undergrowth whatever,— the trees of the noblest height, and just so far apart that horsemen might have galloped in any direction without difficulty. Our driver was a lively intelligent young fellow, having a civil word of inquiry or of greeting for every Indian we encountered: these were by no means numerous however, and they seldom replied by more than a monosyllable, hardly appearing to notice our passage.

The country was in general slightly undulating, but now and then we came to places where I considered us fairly pounded, so abrupt were the declivities and so deep the mud. There are few persons certainly called on for a more frequent display of pluck and coolness than these drivers; I should like some of our flash dragsmen to see one or two bits we got through on this road; not that any mile of it would be considered passable by Pickford's vans, in the condition it was at this season.

We halted for a late breakfast at a solitary log-tavern kept by Americans, where we were received with infinite civility, and where the lady of the *auberge* was inclined to be amiable and communicative,—not an every-day rencontre in these parts. She informed me that the means they could command for the mere necessaries of living were very limited; that butcher's meat was only attainable at Columbus, and that any attempt to rear a stock of poultry was ridiculous, as the Indians of the country invariably stole every feather.

I congratulated her upon the late arrangements of Government, which afforded her the prospect of speedily being rid of these neighbours; but she seemed to think the day of departure was still far distant, not over five hundred having as yet availed themselves of the offers held out to them, although the greater number of those remaining in the country had already disposed of their allotments to speculators and dissipated the money they had received for their land; having neglected to plant an ear of corn, or prepare the least provision for the present winter,—an improvidence of character peculiar to the natives, and which it was, she said, impossible to guard against without depriving them of all free-agency. Many, as she assured me, of these wretched people were at this time suffering from extreme want, and thousands were fast hastening to the like condition, when, unless aided by Government, they must steal or starve.

This poor couple had, as they told me, dwelt in the Indian nation for the last seven years: they seemed decent, industrious folk, yet their habitation bore few marks of growing comfort; the interstices between the logs were unfilled, through these the wind and rain had both free ingress. Their hope, I imagine, was to secure a good allotment of land amongst the improvident sales made by the Indians: they said the place was a good one, and tolerably healthy, excepting in spring and fall; judging by the looks of the family, I should, however, take their estimation of health to be a very low one.

After breakfast the driver made his appearance, and desired us to come down to the stable and fix ourselves as well as we could on the *Box*. Conceiving he alluded to me, I asked if the stage was ready, but received for reply an assurance that it was not intended the stage should be any longer employed on the service; but that, by the agent's order, the *Box* was to be taken on from this point, and that those that liked might go on with it, and those that did not might stay behind.

This was pleasant, but all appeared desirous to trying the *Box*. I confess that a mail conveyance bearing a name so novel excited my curiosity; so, sallying forth, I walked down to the starting-place, where, ready-harnessed and loaded, stood literally the *Box*, made of rough fir plank, eight feet long by three feet wide, with sides two feet deep: it was fixed firmly on an ordinary coach-axle, with pole, &c. The mails and luggage filled the box to overflowing, and on the top of all we were left to, as the driver said, "fix our four quarters in as leetle time as possible."

Now this fixing, in any other part of the globe, would have been deemed an impossibility by persons who were paying for a mail conveyance; but in this spot we knew redress was out of the question—the choice lay between the Box and the forest. We, however, enjoyed the travellers' privilege,—grumbled loudly, cursed all scoundrel stage-agents, who "keep the word of promise to the ear and break it to the hope:" we next laughed at our unavailing ill-humour, which the driver bore with the calmness of a stoic, and finally disposed of our persons as we best could; not the least care having been taken in the disposition of the luggage, our sole care, in fact, was to guard against being jolted off by the movement of the machine; any disposition in favour of ease or comfort was quite out of the question.

During the change, our female companion and her proprietor had walked on; and these were yet to be provided for; however, the sun shone brightly; and we found a subject for congratulation in the fact that rain was not likely to be superadded to our miseries. Short-sighted rogues that we are! What a blessing is it, a knowledge of the evils to come is not permitted to cloud our enjoyments in possession! Crack went the whip. "Hold on with your claws and teeth!" cried the driver; the latter, we found, were only to be kept in the jaws by compression: for the former, we had immediate occasion; our first movement unshipped a trunk and carpet-bag, together with the band-box of our fair passenger—the latter was crushed flat beneath the trunk, and its contents scattered about the way: exposed to the gaze of the profane, lay the whole *materiel* of the toilet of this fair maiden of Sodom. We gathered up a lace cap; ditto of cambric; six love epistles, directed to the lady in as many different hands; a musk-box, and several other indescribable articles; together with an ivory-hilted dagger of formidable proportions, a little sullied, like the maiden's honour, but sharp as a needle. Of the articles enumerated we made a bundle, leaving the shattered band-box on the road. I took the precaution to roll the several billets up in a cambric cap, "guessing" they were not intended for the Colonel's eyes; for so was our male companion styled by the driver.

When we overtook the pair, we made every exertion to dispose of the poor girl, at least securely; who, in truth, merited our cares by the cheerful and uncomplaining spirit she evinced under circumstances full of peril, and ill to bear for the hardiest frame.

Wherever the way permitted a quicker pace than a walk, our condition was really *penible* to a degree; luckily, this did not arrive often, or last long: to crawl at a snail-pace through the mud was now a relief, since one could retain one's seat without straining every muscle to hold on.

Thus we progressed till the evening advanced, when the clouds gathered thick, and then began to roll towards the north-west in dark threatening masses, right in the teeth of a brisk, fitful breeze.

"We'll get it presently," observed our driver, eyeing the drift; "hot as mush, and 'most as thick, by the looks on't."

All at once the wind lulled; then it shifted round to the south-east, and blew out in heavy gusts that bent the tall pines together like rushes: upon this change, lightning quickly followed, playing in the distance about the edge of the darkening horizon. For about two hours we were favoured with these premonitory symptoms, and thus allowed ample time for conjecture as to the probable violence of the storm in active preparation.

Some of our Box crew decided as they desired that it would pass away in threatenings only; others, that all this heralding would be followed by a violent storm, or perhaps by a hurricane. It now occurred to me that, in moments of enthusiasm, encouraged by security, I had expressed myself desirous of witnessing the wild charge of a furious hurricane on the thick ranks of the forest. I confess, however, that, having within the last twenty-four hours witnessed its effects, this desire was considerably abated. With the probable approach of the event, my ardour, like Acre's courage, "oozed away;" and the prospect of such a visitation, whilst exposed on the *Box*, became the reverse of pleasant.

In this uncertainty I resolved to consult our driver's experience; so, coming boldly to the point, demanded,

"I say, driver, do you calculate that we shall be caught in a hurricane?"

"I'll tell you how that'll be exact," replied our oracle: "If the rain comes down pretty, we sha'n't have no hurricane; if it holds up dry, why, we shall."

Henceforth never did ducks pray more devoutly for rain than did the crew of the *Box*, although without hope or thought of shelter; but, on the contrary, with every possible chance of a breakdown or upset, which would have made the forest our bed, but stripped of the "Leaves so green, O!" about which your balladmongers love to sing, with their toes over the fender, and the hail pattering melodiously upon the pantiles. At last, our prayers were heard; and we all, I believe, breathed more freely as the gates of the sky opened, and the falling flood subdued and stilled the hot wind whose heavy gusts rushing among the pines had been the reverse of musical.

The thunder-clouds, hitherto confined to the southern horizon, now closed down upon the forest, deepening its already darkness: at a snail's pace we still proceeded, and luckily found an Indian party encamped close by a sort of bridge lying across a swamp it would have been impossible, as the driver assured us, to have crossed without a good light.

From this party we not only procured a large supply of excellent light-wood, but one of the men heartily volunteered to carry a bundle of it, and act as guide; the squaw of the good fellow was in a violent rage with her man for this courtesy, but he bore her ridicule and reviling with perfect composure. Each of our party carried in his hand a large sliver of this invaluable wood; and, thus prepared, marched in front of the Box across this bridge, almost as ticklish as the single hair leading to Mahomet's heaven: it was a quarter of a mile in length, unguarded by a rail or bulwark of the slighest kind, but generally overhung by the rank growth of the jungle through which it was laid.

My New York companions and I had out-walked the Box; but when about half way across, the rain extinguished our torches, which were rather too slight for the service, when, as we had perceived in our course that many of the planks were unshipped or full of holes, we thought it best to halt for the coming up of our baggage.

I can never forget the effect produced by the blaze of the huge bundle of light wood borne aloft by our Creek guide: I entirely lost sight of the discomfort of our condition in the pleasure I derived from the whole scene.

Let the reader imagine a figure dressed in a deep-yellow shirt reaching barely to the knees, the legs naked; a belt of scarlet wampum about the loins, and a crimson and dark-blue shawl twisted turban-fashion round the head; with locks of black coarse hair streaming from under this, and falling loose over the neck or face: fancy one half of such a figure lighted up by a very strong blaze, marking the nimble tread, the swart cold features, sparkling eye, and outstretched muscular arms of the red-man,—the other half, meantime, being in the blackest possible shadow: whilst following close behind, just perceptible through wreaths of thick smoke, moved the heads of the leading horses; and, over all, flashed at frequent intervals red vivid lightning; one moment breaking forth in a wide sheet, as though an overcharged cloud had burst at once asunder; the next, descending in zigzag lines, or darting through amongst the tall pines and cypress trees; whilst the quick patter of the horses' hoofs were for a time heard loudly rattling over the loose hollow planks, and then again drowned wholly by the crash of near thunder.

Never in my life have I looked upon a scene which holds so vivid a place within my memory: the savage solitude of the jungle, the violence of the storm, together with the pictorial accessories by which the whole picture was kept in movement, fixed the attention, and can never, I think, be forgotten by those who witnessed it.

Having cleared the swamp, we took our places on the Box, still lighted by our friendly Creek; and in about half an hour gained the log-house where the mail agent to whose considerate order we owed our change of vehicle, and consequent added discomfort, dwelt: here, however, a clean comfortable meal of tea, chops, fowls, and hot bread of every denomination awaited us.

My first movement on jumping off the Box was to lay hands on the Indian guide, and to proffer to him a flask of cognac, which had proved of singular comfort to the party: to my great surprise, he at once declined tasting it; smiling and pointing his finger to his forehead, he gravely repeated half a dozen words, which a by-stander of the nation readily translated to mean,—"Whisky water make man not eat,—bad for sore head."

I agreed with this as a general rule, but at the same time begged my Creek to look on old brandy as an exception, when used medicinally; this being duly interpreted, the Indian laughed heartily, but abided by his rejection of the consolation. During our parley he took the red and blue shawl from off his head, wrung it as dry as possible, refolded it, and then adjusted his turban with infinite care, preparing forthwith to be gone: he did not depart without a slight gratuity, and took with him our best wishes. This was a fine open-countenanced fellow, middle-sized, and firmly built; he was, in fact, one of the few really good-looking aborigines I have met. As he was departing from the house, I asked if he did not require a bundle of light-wood to show him his road home; he laughed, and replied, "No, he was no wagon; no fear of him falling into the swamp."

Away he dashed into the mud at a quick trot, with bent knees and folded arms, anxious, I fancied, to appease his squaw; since it was contrary to her desire that he had ventured on this service, and not, as the coachman assured us, without receiving much abuse for his foolishness, as his "gentle ladye" termed this courtesy.

Here we learned that the mail preceding us had been over-turned into a stream from off the bridge we had next to pass, and lay there yet; luckily no passenger was in it at the time: our new driver added, that he had no expectations of getting the coach through, but he was bound to try. So wearied were we, that any or all of the party would have been well contented to stay here; but no place could be given us to sleep in, and until the next coach passed, no means could be procured to forward us to Montgom-ery; we had no choice therefore but to push on with the mail and meet our fortune.

From this hour, midnight, until daylight, we were generally on foot; the driver in one or two instances refusing to advance until even the poor girl got out, assuring us that he would not hazard the young woman's life, however hard it was for her to face the night and the roads, frequently over knee-deep.

We had a plentiful supply of fire-wood: we were able, and, I will add, willing men; and by dint of great personal exertion, added to an excellent team, and a judicious driver, we brought the coach through all difficulties, arriving at Montgomery at six in the morn-ing: thus completing a journey of ninety miles in thirty-two hours; and having paid well to be permitted to assist in getting the mail-bag through roads which, for the next few days, remained, I be-lieve utterly impassable, even under the circumstances I have here attempted to describe.

At Montgomery we found a wretched inn, with no possibility of procuring anything save liquor; but we had the good luck to learn that in a couple of hours a steam-boat was departing for Mobile, down the Alabama: we gave up the stage therefore, and sallied out of this den of a hotel for the steamer Carolina. This

movement was lucky, as the stage-route to Mobile was, as I afterwards learned, as bad as the worst we had come through; all the
late coaches had met with accidents, and the added rain of the last
twenty-four hours would, it was presumed, render it impassable.

I was so wearied that I saw little of this place but a muddy
river, whose banks were strewn with bales of cotton awaiting the
means of transport. I could hardly keep my eyes open till I had
swallowed my breakfast: a clean-looking berth was assigned me,
and, turning in, I remained oblivious to the world and its cares
until after noon of the following day, when I awoke fresh as a bird
and hungry as an ostrich.

12

George William Featherstonhaugh
January 1835

※

ENGLISH-BORN GEORGE WILLIAM FEATHERSTONHAUGH (1780-1866) CAME TO THE UNITED STATES AS A YOUNG MAN. THE WAR DEPARTMENT APPOINTED HIM UNITED STATES GEOLOGIST, AND IN 1834-35 HE SURVEYED THE WESTERN TERRITORIES. SUBSEQUENTLY THE BRITISH GOVERNMENT COMMISSIONED HIM TO HELP IN SETTLING THE BOUNDARY DISPUTE BETWEEN GREAT BRITAIN AND THE UNITED STATES. HAVING SUCCESSFULLY SERVED IN THAT CAPACITY, THE BRITISH GOVERNMENT APPOINTED HIM AS ONE OF ITS CONSELS IN FRANCE.

FEATHERSTONHAUGH'S PUBLICATIONS—WHICH FOCUS ON GEOLOGICAL, STATISTICAL AND POLITICAL SUBJECTS—EXHIBIT THE OBJECTIVITY OF THE SCIENTIFIC MIND.

George William Featherstonhaugh. *Excursion through the Slave States, from Washington on the Potomac to the Frontier of Mexico; with Sketches of Popular Manners and Geological Notices.* New York: Harper and Brothers, 1844. Pages 145-153.

There was little temptation to remain here [Montgomery], and I turned my attention to leaving the place as soon as I found out how uncomfortable it was likely to be. Upon inquiry I found that the roads through the Indian territory of the Creek nation, through which I had now to pass to get into the State of Georgia, were excessively broken up, especially the Indian bridges which cross the great swamps, and that in consequence thereof the letters were

99

forwarded on horseback, the mail-stage being unable to run; so
that I had got into a cleft stick, and must either remain here until
the roads became passable for the mail—which was not expected
until spring—or must take a private conveyance and pay any price
they might think proper to exact of me. The landlord was the person I had to deal with, and he ended a monstrous account of the
difficulties with an equally monstrous price for conducting us in a
miserable vehicle and a pair of wretched horses to Columbus, in
Georgia, the distance being ninety miles. After a good deal of chaf-
fering, I finally agreed to give him sixty-five dollars, which, with
a gratuity to the driver, amounted to about four shillings a mile in
English money.

Instead of getting off early the next morning as had been agreed,
everything had to be repaired; but at length, to our great satisfac-
tion, we got out of the filthy house into the pine woods, where a
gentle air was mournfully but pleasingly rustling the branches.
We found the road as we advanced quite answering to the description they had given us of it, being so frightfully cut up as to render
it impossible to sit in the vehicle: wherever it was dry enough,
therefore, we walked, expecting every instant to see the carriage
overturned; and indeed the manner in which it survived the rolling
from one side to the other was quite surprising. The black fellow,
however, who drove us, seemed to take it as philosophically as if
there was nothing uncommon in this sort of motion; he always
urged us in a very anxious manner to get in whenever he came up
with us, and seemed to think we were not quite right in our senses
for preferring to walk when we paid so much for riding. At length
we came to a low part of the country completely inundated, where
it was impossible to walk, the water being in many places four
feet deep. Here we were obliged to get in, and the old vehicle took
to rolling in such a dreadful manner that every instant we expected
to be soused into the water; and what rendered it really amusing
was, that we were constantly obliged to draw up our limbs on the
seat, for the water was at least eight inches deep in the bottom of
the carriage, and went splashing about in the most extraordinary
manner. All this time our trunks, which were lashed on behind,

were being quietly dragged under the water. Mine had got such a satisfactory ducking before I had time to think of it, that I turned my attention exclusively to my portfolio and instruments to prevent them from getting wet, casting a look now and then at my companion, who never having travelled in that style in his native mountains, looked very woe-begone, and was constantly exclaiming, "Mais quel pays! A-t-on jamais vu de pareils chemins?" Fatigued and wet, we reached at night an old settler's of the name of M'Laughlin, a very respectable sort of man, who lived upon some of the land which the Creeks had been compelled to surrender. In the course of the day we had only made fourteen miles, and the whole performance had been of such an anomalous character, that, persuaded it could not have been got up for less than that money in any other part of the world, I became quite reconciled to the landlord and his four shillings a mile.

Next morning we went five miles to *Oakfuskee* Creek to breakfast, a pretty brawling stream, forming the present boundary betwixt the Creeks and the State of Alabama, which we crossed in a ferry boat. We were now upon Indian territory, still possessed by the Indians, and where the laws, manners, and customs of the whites did not yet prevail. Captivated in my youth by what I had read and heard of the aboriginal inhabitants of North America, I had been led to visit that continent as early as 1806, more for the purpose of seeing the tribes of red men, and studying their languages, than with any other view, and in the succeeding year had visited most of the tribes in Upper and Lower Canada, with others dwelling within the limits of the United States. The insight I had obtained into the anomalous structure of the Indian dialects, which is to the ear what the synthetic arrangement of Chinese written characters is to the eye, had induced me to seek for information respecting the Cherokee and Muskogee, or Creek tongues; and thus becoming familiar with the history of those people, I could not but feel a deep interest in the present state of the Creeks, to which they had been brought by a series of events that made them deserving of sympathy and admiration.

———

    The Muskogee, or Creek people, are not to be considered as a dull, imbecile race of aboriginal savages, with not an idea beyond that of supplying their daily wants: they rather resemble the Suliots, or some of those communities of Asiatic people, who, passionately attached to their native country, have contended with the most desperate valour to preserve it from the invaders whom they hated. Inhabiting an ardent climate, and a fertile country which supplied all their wants, war and the chase, at the period when the whites first appeared amongst them, were the pursuits they exclusively gave themselves up to. To powerful frames and forms of great symmetry, they united activity of person and undaunted courage. Their copper-coloured complexions, long coarse black hair, and dark wild eyes, were the *beau ideal* of Indian beauty; and perhaps no human being could be more remarkable than a young, well-made Creek warrior on horseback, dressed in a gaudy calico hunting-shirt, with a bright-coloured silk handkerchief wound gracefully round his head in the form of a turban.

    Previous to the year 1790 the Muskogee population was very great, and claimed dominion over and possessed a territory, bounded on the east by the Savannah river, which comprehended perhaps twenty-five millions of acres of fertile land, being more than three-fourths of the whole area of England. But about that period, the population of the State of Georgia encroaching continually upon them, they found it necessary to enter into negotiations with the general government of the United States, then administered by President Washington.

    At this time Alexander M'Gillivray was, as he had long been, the principal chief of the Creek people. He was the son of an Englishman by a Creek woman, had been well educated at Charlestan [sic.] in South Carolina, and was fifty years old. At the death of his mother, who was herself a half-breed, he became first sachem by the usages of the nation; but leaving it to the people whether that dignity should be continued in his hands, they not only insisted upon his retaining that rank, but afterwards called him, as if by general consent, "king of kings;" and, from all the accounts we have of him, he was universally beloved by the people, and deserved their attachment. During the civil war between Great Britain and her colonies, he adhered to the mother country, and fought against the Americans; but, after the peace, circumstances occurring which made it doubtful whether a collision might not take place between the Georgians and his people, he was invited by the federal authorities to New York, where the seat of government then was; and going there with other chiefs in 1790, was well received by President Washington, with whose government he concluded a treaty in the month of August of that year. This treaty was the first of *twelve* that have been made by the United States with the Muskogee nation, and each of them has been a *treaty of cession* except the last. In all the others the Creeks have gradually been made to cede a portion of their country adjoining to their neighbours the Georgians, and to fall back upon the remainder; in each case that remainder being *solemnly guaranteed to them* by the United States. The tenth treaty left them a very limited portion of their ancient country; but by the eleventh they ceded every foot of land contained in that limited portion. By the twelfth and last treaty, the United States government stipulate to give them certain lands west of the Mississippi for their nation to inhabit for ever; that is to say, until the white population shall reach them, when the same game will have necessarily to be played over again.

In the first treaty, made in the year 1790, are the two following articles:

"Art. 5. The United States *solemnly guarantee* to the Creek nation all their lands within the limits of the United States, to the westward and southward of the boundary described by the preceding article.

"Art. 6. If any citizen of the United States, or other person, not being an Indian, shall attempt to settle on any of the Creek lands, such person shall forfeit the protection of the United States; *and the Creeks may punish him or not, as they please.*"

The manner in which the guarantee in the fifth article has been observed, is sufficiently explained by the fact that by the succeeding treaties the Creeks have ceded every foot of land they possessed; and as to the sixth article, which provides that the Creeks may punish intruders upon their lands, it was expressly because they endeavoured to enforce this article, and prevent new intruders settling upon their lands, that new quarrels arose betwixt them and the Georgians, which always ended in a new treaty and an important cession of the land intruded upon, under the pretence, generally, that it was within the "chartered rights of Georgia."

If the Creeks, however, had remained a united people in their resistance to these encroachments, the spoliation of their territory would not have proceeded so rapidly. Unfortunately they became divided amongst themselves by the arts of the white men, and, as has often occurred in similar cases, the party that maintained the independence of the nation was opposed by a minority, jealous of the ascendancy of some of the chiefs, and which rashly sought to strengthen itself by the counsels and aid of the white men, whose sole object was to eject them all from the country.

As early as 1790 this became a source of weakness to the nation. M'Gillivray in his treaty of that period, had made an important cession of territory to the United States, upon the ostensible consideration of an annuity of 1500 dollars, and a present of "certain valuable Indian goods." This was represented as an act of treason to his nation; it was said that he had been corrupted, had become a pensioner of the United States, and had ceded a part of their territory without the consent of a general council of the people. The Sachem was so much hurt by the opposition he met with on his return, that he left his nation for awhile, and went to the Spanish settlements, from whence, however, he returned, and appeared for a time to have recovered his popularity; probably this was only in appearance, for he again went to Florida, and died at Pensacola in 1793.

By the treaty of November 14, 1805, another very important cession of territory was made to the United States, together with a right to a *horse path* throughout the whole Creek territory, "in such direction as shall, by the President of the United States, be considered most convenient," with a right to all Americans to pass peaceably thereon, the Creek chiefs stipulating to keep ferry-boats at the rivers for "the conveyance of men and horses." In this treaty, which threw the whole Creek territory open to the whites, nothing is said about the right of the Creeks to punish intruders on their lands; but the United States agreed to give to the nation 12,000 dollars, in money or goods, for the term of eight years, and 11,000 dollars, in money or goods, for the term of the ten succeeding years, without interest.

The work of plunder and corruption was now rising to a great height; the increasing population of Georgia was pressing upon the Indians, and the legislature of that State—in which the speculators upon Indian lands had a predominating influence—carried its political weight to the Congress to effect these treaties that were to aggrandize their own State and satisfy the rapacity of their own citizens, who were the speculators and politicians for whose benefit these treaties were to be made. At all times there have been honourable and just men in the Congress, who saw into these machinations, and opposed them, but always in vain; and the executive government, who perceived how irresi[s]tibly events were tending to accomplish the absorption of all the lands which had been so solemnly guaranteed to the Indians, could do no more, even if it were otherwise disposed, that to modify the injustice which was perpetrating, by executing the treaties as impartially as circumstances admitted of. Every thing seemed to concur to nourish the increasing passion of the Americans to appropriate all territories that were contiguous to them, and to create an extravagant opinion in the minds of the rising generations, that there was no moral impropriety in any claim made by the United States, as they could not by any possibility be in the wrong. The chiefs of the Upper Creek nation, who immediately adjoined the Americans—the Judases who had betrayed their country—and through whose hands these annuities passed, became now, many of them, as eager to earn these pensions by the destruction of their nation, as the Georgians were to encourage them; they had their own friends to reward, and the fruits of their treachery being soon dissipated in whiskey and personal indulgences, their partisans became clamorous for the means of gratifying their propensities.

On the other hand the *Lower Creeks*, who had not tasted so abundantly the sweets of these treaties of peace and friendship, were becoming more and more estranged from the upper nation; and when the United States declared war against Great Britain in 1812, they took up arms against the Americans, and led by

Weatherford—one of those half-breeds that are sometimes gifted with such a surprising degree of eloquence, courage, and resources, as raises them at once to be the leaders of their nation—performed acts as conspicuous for their daring as they were for savage ferocity. Amongst these was the surprisal of Fort Mimms, a fort built by the United States in the Creek territory. At the head of 1500 warriors Weatherford boldly attacked the fort at noonday. Major Beasley, the Commandant, had a garrison in it of 275 persons, some of whom were women and children. He had been already apprised of the approach of Weatherford; and if he had taken proper precautions, could, with about 200 men that he had under his command, have effectually resisted the attack. Despising his enemy, he appears to have strangely neglected the safety of the fort, which gave Weatherford an opportunity of surprising it before they had time to close the gates, at which point a most sanguinary contest took place hand to hand. The Americans fought bravely, and disputed the entrance with desperate valour: they were however unable to close the gates [which were blocked by sand], and a furious contest of swords, bayonets, knives, and tomahawks, at length terminated in favour of the Indians, the brave Major Beasly and his gallant brother officers being every one slain on the spot. Having massacred the garrison, the Indians set fire to the blockhouses where the women and children had taken refuge, and, with the exception of a few, burnt them all up. Of the whole number of 275, only 17 survived, some of whom were severely wounded.

The news of this disastrous affair caused a great excitement in the states that were conterminous with the Indian territory. Amongst these was the State of Tennessee, which bordered upon the Cherokee and Creek lands; and as this success was considered to be of a very dangerous character, since it might lead to a combination of all the Indian tribes, most of whom would willingly have entered into a general war, it was determined to oppose to Weatherford a man whose reputation for courage and determination was at that time well established in his own State. This man was the now celebrated General Jackson, who, being highly popular in Tennessee, soon succeeded in raising 2000 fighting men, equipped for Indian warfare, and burning to retaliate upon the Indians the destruction of the garrison of Fort Mimms. General Jackson soon took the field before a regular commissariat could be established, crossed the Tennessee River, and trusting often to casual supplies, plunged into the wild country drained by the Black Warrior and Coosa rivers. On his left were a party of the upper Creeks, friendly to the United States, under the command of another famous half-breed named William M'Intosh, who, being bitterly opposed to Weatherford and the lower Creeks, sought every opportunity to damage them. Such was the fury of this man against his own countrymen, that at the battle of Autossee—a place on the south bank of the Tallapoosa, about twenty miles north of east from Montgomery—he assisted most ferociously in the massacre of 200 wretched Creeks, who were surprised in their wigwams.

After a great many fights in which the Creeks were uniformly defeated and sustained severe losses, they were induced by their prophets to fortify themselves upon a neck of land formed by a great curve in the Tallapoosa River, which the Creeks call *Tohopeka*, or Horse-Shoe. In this desperate state of their affairs the poor Indians clung with more than their accustomed confidence to the conjurers of their nation who pretended to divine the future, and who had assumed the title of prophets. They were assured that this was the place where they were to conquer, and at any rate it was evident, from what was observed after the battle, that the last struggle was intended to be made here. They had fortified themselves with great ingenuity, the points of resistance afforded by the locality were very favourable to them, and having about 1000 tried men, they were not afraid of being taken by storm.

Here Jackson followed them. His army had repeatedly mutinied for want of provisions, and he only kept it together by sharing in an unostentatious manner all the privations of his men; making no regular repasts, but sustaining himself by the grains of corn which he carried in his pocket, and which he sometimes offered to his men when they were sinking from weakness and fatigue. With such an example in the chief, soldiers with any generous feelings will follow wherever he leads them. As soon as he reached the place where the wretched Creeks—themselves undergoing every sort of privation—were about to play their last stake, he attacked the place with a settled purpose to finish the war at this point. In his official letter he says, "*Determined to exterminate them*, I detached General Coffee with the mounted and nearly the whole of the Indian force early in the morning of yesterday [March 27th, 1814], to cross the river about two miles below their encampment, and to surround the bend in such a manner *as that none of them should escape* by attempting to cross the river." The place, after a severe contest of five hours, was stormed, and the Americans entered it. Five hundred and fifty-seven Indians were slain on the bend, and many others who attempted to cross the Tallapoosa were sabred by the horsemen; but to pursue the official letter—"The fighting continued with some severity about five hours, but we continued to destroy many of them who had concealed themselves under the banks of the river until we were prevented by night. *This morning we killed sixteen who had been concealed.* We took about 250 prisoners, all women and children, except two or three. Our loss is 106 wounded, and 25 killed. Major M'Intosh, the Cowetau, who joined my army with a part of his tribe, greatly distinguished himself."

If it had been a den of rattlesnakes their destruction could not have been accomplished or related in a more energetic manner.

Some of the Creeks now fled to Florida, and others into the Cherokee country, whilst Weatherford and the few Indians adhered to him, were hunted into the swamps, and hemmed in such a manner as to be reduced to the last extremity, feeding upon the roots and the barks of trees until famine and disease rapidly diminished their numbers. In the meantime Jackson had required of the Indians who adhered to the Americans to cause that chief to be delivered bound to him to undergo his fate. Weatherford soon received information of this, and unable any longer to endure the misery of his followers, and determined not to submit to the indignity of being bound, he resolved upon a step that marks the elevation of his character, and that produced consequences that reflect great honour even upon the successful American general.

It happened to me many years ago to hear the relation of what took place from an eye-witness of the first interview which Weatherford had with his conqueror.

Jackson was one day in his tent with some of his officers, when an Indian was seen on horseback galloping into the encampment, and who did not stop until he reached the General's tent. Throwing himself from his horse, he entered the tent boldly, and in a moment stood before the commander-in-chief. The Indian was tall and well-proportioned, his countenance indicated great intelligence, and was distinguished by that particular beauty which is sometimes given by a thin aquiline nose. His person was squalid and emaciated, his dress dirty and ragged, but his brilliant and still fierce black eyes showed at once that he was no common man. Addressing himself to Jackson, he instantly began to this effect:—

"I am Weatherford; I fought you as long as I could; I can fight no longer; my people are dying in the swamp. Do with *me* as you please; I give myself up. I know you are a brave man; have pity on my people. Let them have something to eat; send a good talk to them; they will do what you wish. Here I am."

The inexorable temper of Jackson was softened by the abject condition of the fallen chief, and his generosity awakened by this heroic conduct: he spoke kindly to Weatherford, and bade him be comforted, declaring with warmth that no man should hurt a hair of his head, and that if the Indians would submit, he would take care of them and give them peace. Thus did this generous step, which could only have been suggested by a lofty mind, produce the happiest effects.

The Creeks had now received a fatal blow both to their power and their pride. They were at the mercy of their conquerors, and on the 9th of August, 1814, signed articles of "Agreement and Capitulation" with the successful General at Fort Jackson. These articles began as follows:—"Whereas an *unprovoked*, inhuman, and sanguinary war, waged by the hostile Creeks against the United States, hath been repelled, prosecuted, and determined successfully on the part of the said States, *in conformity with principles of national justice* and honourable warfare," &c.

By this treaty the Creeks ceded every part of the territory that was required of them. All the upper part of the Coosa country was surrendered, and that river as far as Wetumpka became their boundary. Within the space of twenty-four years the Creeks had now surrendered—with a few local exceptions—all that portion of their native country extending from the Coosa eastward to the Savannah; comprehending about 250 miles in breadth of the finest land in the United States. But a fine territory was still left to them, and if there was any virtue in words, the United States were bound by the following article in the treaty to protect them in its possession:—

"Art. 2. The United States *will guarantee* to the Creek nation the integrity of all their territory eastwardly and northwardly of the said line, to be run and described as mentioned in the first article."

Further concessions, however, were made by the treaty of January 22, 1818, in consideration of the United States paying the sum of 120,000 dollars, in certain instalments; and on the 8th of January, 1821, a subsequent treaty of cession took place for other valuable considerations.

William M'Intosh, the half breed, who had contributed so effectually to the destruction of his countrymen, the lower Creeks, was now the leading Sachem, and was the chief under whose management these treaties of cession were made. Emboldened by his success, and urged on by the speculators who were still watching for opportunities to despoil the nation of everything, he now ventured upon a proceeding which roused the lower Creeks from their apathy, and signed a convention, February 12, 1825, with certain American commissioners who were Georgians, in which it was provided that a further important cession should be made to the United States, for which the parties interested were to be compensated in the following manner. They were to receive acre for acre upon the Arkansas River, west of the Mississippi, upon condition of their emigrating to that country, and were besides to be paid a sum amounting to *four hundred thousand dollars* in money, to compensate them for their losses in removing from their native country and to enable them "to obtain supplies in their new settlement."

The Creeks had submitted with impatient reluctance to the previous cession made by M'Intosh, but this, which expatriated a great portion of them into the bargain, was intolerable. In vain had the chiefs told the American commissioners, at a council to which they were summoned, "We have no land to sell. M'Intosh knows that no part of the land can be sold without a full council, and with the consent of all the nation; and if a part of the nation choose to leave the country, they cannot sell the land they have, but it belongs to the nation." A deaf ear was turned to this, and M'Intosh, tempted by the personal advantages that were to be secured to him, and believing that the United States government would carry out the execution of the treaty, signed the document, with a few of the chiefs connected with him, whilst thirty-six of them, present at the council, refused to put their marks to it. Many of the chiefs now openly denounced him; and letters he had written to some of the half-breeds, offering to bribe them with part of the money he was to receive from the American commissioners, being produced at a subsequent council, his treachery to the nation was apparent to every one. Perceiving that a great majority of the Creeks were inclined against him, M'Intosh repaired to the State of Georgia, where his abettors were, and claimed the protection of the governor [McIntosh's cousin, Governor Troup]. Having been assured that he should receive it, he returned to his house, on the Chatahoochie, where two of his wives lived, and where some Americans and sub-chiefs of his own party soon joined him. While here, relying upon the powerful protection of Governor Troup of Georgia, Menaw-way, a chief of the lower country, accompanied by a very large party of armed Oakfuskee warriors, suddenly surrounded the house on Sunday morning the 1st of May, about two hours before daylight. As soon as day broke he sent an interpreter to inform the white people in the house that they and the women and children must instantly leave it; that it was not his intention to hurt them, but that General M'Intosh having broken the law of the nation, they intended to execute him immediately. All now left the house but M'Intosh and one Tustenugge, who was his principal confederate in executing the obnoxious treaties. Menaw-way, who seemed determined to hold no conversation with the delinquent chiefs, now directed his warriors to set fire to the house; and the inmates, making a desperate sally from the door to escape being burnt alive, were both shot dead.

The governor of Georgia, incensed at this execution of his protégés, breathed nothing but vengeance against their enemies, who, probably, but for the wise and humane view which the federal government (then administered by President Adams) took of the causes which had led to this characteristic and summary proceeding, would have had to undergo new persecutions from their white neighbours. The President not only used his authority upon this occasion to protect the Indians from further injury, but entered into a treaty with them on 24th of January, 1826, whereby the last convention signed by M'Intosh was declared null and void. This treaty contained also a cession of some lands, to make it acceptable to the Georgians, for which the sum of 217,600 dollars was to be paid to the chiefs and warriors, as well as an additional perpetual annuity of 20,000 dollars. The interests also of the friends of M'Intosh were provided for; they were to emigrate to the west side of the Mississippi—an arrangement which met their approbation—and were to be liberally provided for, and to be under the protection of the United States. This treaty, which was no doubt made in a spirit of fairness to the Indians, also contained the usual *guarantee* to all the lands "not herein ceded, to which they have a just claim." A further treaty of cession, however, was entered into on the 25th of November, 1827, for the purpose of quieting some titles in the "chartered limits of Georgia," the sum of 42,000 dollars being the consideration paid by the United States.

The last treaty of cession was made on the 24th of March, 1832, when the government of the United States was administered by President Jackson, the person who had given the Creeks such a fatal blow in 1814. The treaty commenced in the following significant words:

"Art. 1. The Creek tribe of Indians cede to the United States *all their land east of the Mississippi river.*"

Thus was extinguished the title of the Muskogee people to every foot of land comprehended in their ancient territory, consisting of about twenty-five millions of acres of fertile land, all of which had been now ceded in a little more than forty years to the white population of the adjacent States.

The speculators had now effected their great object of despoiling the Creeks of their native country. Ostensibly, the treaty provided for the interests of the Indians, but, substantially, it was a provision for their plunderers. Ninety of the principal chiefs were to have one section* (640 acres) of land each, as soon as the survey of the land had been effected by the United States; and every head of a Creek family was also to have a half section. Those who consented to emigrate and join their countrymen west of the Mississippi were to be removed at the expense of the American government, and to be subsisted by it one year after their arrival there. To the speculators the most interesting portion of the treaty was contained in the following words:

"Art. 3. The tracts [those provided for the chiefs and heads of families] may be conveyed by the persons selecting the same *to any other persons, for a fair consideration*, in such manner as the President may direct."

Now these chiefs and heads of families, thus to be provided for, were illiterate, wretched beings, broken down in spirit by the ruin of their nation, and most of them addicted to excessive drunkenness. There was not a part of the territory where white men were not to be found vending whiskey to the poor Indians on credit; so that at the time this treaty was made they were all deeply indebted; or if any of them had had but slight dealings with these men, being entirely illiterate, they neither knew how to keep an account of their transactions, nor what the nature of the paper was which they had been induced to sign before witnesses on coming to a settlement.

So degraded and miserable was their condition, that almost any of them could be brought to sign any thing when sufficiently excited by whiskey; and although the third article provided that the conveyance of their lands to others should be made under the direction of the President, yet he could do no more than delegate agents to inquire into the transactions of the Indians and their white creditors, which agents were always presumed to be favourable to these last, and to be easily satisfied of the "fair consideration" that had been given. Substantially, therefore, this treaty was a liquidation of accounts betwixt them and their creditors, and transferred to these last the lands which it ostensibly assigned to the Indians: indeed if any of them had even succeeded in retaining possession of their sections, it was evident, that under such a state of things it was impossible for isolated individuals to live amongst the white men that were now about to pour in amongst them: they could follow the chase no longer, all their occupations were at an end, and nothing would soon be left for them but acts of violence and drunkenness, until disease should destroy them, or until they should be forcibly removed from the country. Such was the situation, and such the future prospects, of the remains of the great Muskogee people at the ratification of this treaty.

It is due, however, to truth to say that there had never been wanting virtuous and excellent persons in other parts of the United States to inveigh loudly against the whole system of proceedings by which such an atrocious spoliation was consummated. Nearer to the scene of action a more moderate degree of disapprobation was sometimes expressed, and it was not unusual to hear a qualified apology for these transactions from sensible and respectable persons, who would shrink from committing acts of injustice and inhumanity themselves; and who observed that, however criminal such proceedings might appear, the removal of Indians from their lands did not attach as a crime to the nation that removed them; for where the white population increased so rapidly, the necessity of their removal became unavoidable; and the act, therefore, being involuntary, could not be a crime.

If a contrast were to be drawn between the intrinsic importance to the world, of a nation of aboriginal savages and a community of civilized and religious white people, all men would probably be found to agree which of the two should be preserved, even if it involved the destruction of the other. In the eyes of the educated white man, the life of the Indian is divested of every rational comfort, that could encourage him to hope he could ever be reconciled to it. It is a mere animal life, without religion, and without any law except the law of revenge. Restrained neither by education nor example, passion alone rules, and war and the chase become his sole occupations. His children pursue the savage customs of their forefathers; and as they increase in numbers, only extend the deadly spectacle of whole nations living and dying without the desire of knowledge. With a well-trained white man, every thing is in a state of religious and moral progression. Education engrafts the desire of knowledge in his young mind, and renders its acquisition certain. His labour, successfully applied in one direction, opens other avenues to him still more profitable, and leads to the development of every recourse of human talent and ingenuity. He abounds in the substantial comforts of life, and is the friend of peace and law, knowing that they alone furnish a secure protection to the future enjoyment by his generations of the property he has acquired by his own honourable labours. We may believe, therefore, that men who thus, by their sobriety, industry, fidelity, and integrity in social life, exemplify a consciousness of their responsibility to their Creator, are, whilst extending their generations, worthily pursuing the true purposes of their existence, are qualifying themselves for a more perfect state of enjoyment hereafter, such, perhaps, as we can hardly conceive the mere animal Indian to be capable of aspiring to. This contrast, however, if it is not altogether theoretical, is not by any means applicable to the people of Georgia. They, at any rate, were not under the necessity of expelling the Creeks to make room for an increasing virtuous population: their proceedings had been at all times marked by fraud and violence, against which their victims had in vain looked up for protection to the federal government,—a protection it was bound upon every consideration, divine and human, to have given them, and which, perhaps, it was alone restrained from doing by sordid political management. If the federal government could not have done every thing the Creeks could fairly claim under its repeated solemn guarantees, there was still something left in its power. Having repeatedly treated with them as an independent people under their protection, it was bound to give them a domestic government, to have provided for their conversion to Christianity, and to have afforded them every facility of becoming cultivators, and forming themselves into contented communities, as some of the Choctaws and Cherokees are at this day.

With these events, as they are just sketched, uppermost in my mind, I now entered the Creek territory. The lands had been surveyed, the chiefs who had deluded the nation into the treaty had been well provided for, and the rest, with very few exceptions, had transferred their rights to white men. I was now to be a witness, not of the ruins of a Palmyra or a Babylon, but of a nation of famous warriors degraded to the lowest pitch of drunkenness and despair, and surrounded in every direction by the least industrious and most dissolute white men on the continent of America.

Everything as we advanced was Indian, the road was crooked, bad, and made without any system, and by its side occasional ragged-looking pieces of ground, badly cleared up, on which were built miserable-looking cabins without any fences near them. We had not been half an hour in the territory before we came to a filthy cabin where a villanous-looking white man sold tobacco and whiskey. A stream was running close by, and at the door of the cabin three other brutal-looking whites were standing with this man, all engaged in making game of a fine tall Indian, about forty-five years old, who was remarkably well made. He was excessively drunk, and was staggering about stark naked and vociferating in an unintelligible manner, whilst the foam from his mouth was falling on his prominent breast. These fellows were promising him another drink if he would jump into the stream, but although they had persuaded him to strip, the morning was so cold and the water—on account of the late rains—so high, that he seemed to have sense enough left not to go any farther. We left the place thoroughly disgusted, but I have no doubt they prevailed upon him at length, for the Indian, when tipsy, is outrageous for more liquor until he becomes dead drunk; and the men told us that he had often done it before. Our road was indescribably bad, going over beds of black waxy plastic clay, of the consistency of that on the small prairies in Arkansas, and entirely cut up by the immense number of waggons containing families that were emigrating from South Carolina to Alabama. Being on foot, and always ahead of the carriage, I used to enter the Indian cabins I came up with, and enter into conversation with those of the people who could speak a little English. Nothing could exceed the dirt and stench of these places. In one of them I stopped half an hour, and saw breakfast cooked for some Indian women by a negress who was their slave; it consisted of some rotten-looking meat, and her manner of cooking it, in a dirty pan which seemed never to have been cleaned, was something quite shocking.

On reaching the Kateebee swamp we found the bridge of logs, which extended about a mile, quite dislocated with the incessant passage of waggons and the rise of the waters. A file of them had just passed it with great difficulty, and on taking a look at the numerous holes made in it, some of which were four feet deep, I despaired of getting our vehicle over. A person on horseback, who was accompanying one of the waggons, and with whom I had entered into conversation, very kindly lent me his horse to cross the swamp with, and gave me directions how to proceed; by observing these I succeeded, after a hard struggle; and on reaching the other end, where were some more waggons, I sent the horse back to him by a negro slave belonging to one of them.

Almost the whole of the bridge was under water, and in one part of it the structure had been quite broken up for a distance of at least 200 yards, the horse treading fearfully amongst the logs, some of which were floating and some sticking in the mud, not a little puzzled how to get out of these chasms after I had forced him into them.

From hence I proceeded on foot to Walton's, a house of entertainment, where the carriage finally overtook me, to the great satiasfaction of Mr. T********, who considered the log-bridge, when he got upon it, as the *ne plus ultra* of his travels in this direction; but the driver was accustomed to scenes of this kind, and telling him to sit still, at length extricated him. At this house I met two ladies, both of them very genteel persons, on their way from Charlestown, in South Carolina, to Mobile: one of them was a Mrs. H*****, and the other was a Mrs. B****, her niece, an extremely beautiful and interesting young person, who had lately been left a widow. Having heard unpromising accounts of the Kateebee Swamp, they had stopped here to get information from some one who had crossed it. We took a late repast together, and I do not know that I ever felt more sympathy for any individuals than for these amiable women, who were travelling through such an inhospitable country at this unpropitious season, with no attendants but a boy and a negro who drove their carriage. On parting I gave him instructions how to proceed, and was glad to find he was an intelligent and careful man. As to his fair charge, they were both resolutely bent upon making the best of everything, and were prepared to meet events in that admirable spirit which frequently characterizes the sex upon perilous occasions.

Everything as we advanced into the Creek country announced the total dissolution of order. Indians of all ages were wandering about listlessly, the poorest of them having taken to begging, and when we came in sight would come and importune us for money. Some of them, imitating the whites, were doing their best to prey upon each other, for we frequently saw squaws belonging to some of the chiefs seated by the roadside at a log or rude table with a bottle of whiskey, and a glass to supply their unfortunate countrymen who had anything to give in return, if it were only the skin of an animal. These women seemed to laugh at the distresses of the others, and gave us a great deal of their eloquence when we passed them, but fortunately we did not understand what they said, though by their lifting up the whiskey bottle it was evident they wanted to make something out of us also. In other places we met young men in the flower of their age, dressed in ragged hunting-shirts and turbans, staggering along, and often falling to the ground, with empty bottles in their hands: in this wretched state of things, with the game almost entirely destroyed, it is evident that nothing will soon be left to those who have beggared themselves but to die of want, or to emigrate, a step they are so very averse to take, that in their desperation they have already committed some murders.

The jurisdiction of this part of the territory had now passed over from the United States to the State of Alabama, which not having yet commenced its exercise, the Indians did just as they pleased. One of them lately shot a sort of itinerant preacher, named Davis, with whom he had had some dealings, and afterwards came to Walton's and said he was very sorry, but he thought it was a wild turkey he had fired at. This no doubt was a piece of Indian wit, and meant not that he was sorry for what he had done, but that he was sorry it was not a wild turkey he had shot. The few white families who have established themselves on the road were beginning, and with reason, to be alarmed at their situation, for it would require very little combination on the part of the Indians to massacre them all in one night.

At the Persimmon Creek and Swamp we met with another broken-down log bridge that was dangerous in some places; but several Indians who were here behaved very well, giving us most effectual assistance in getting the carriage across, for which we paid them liberally. From hence we proceeded to one Macgirt's a white man, living in a filthy, Indian-looking place, who pretended to give us some breakfast, but it was so disgustingly bad that we were unable to touch it. This man said he expected every night to have his throat cut, which induced me to tell him, that if it would be any consolation, he might be quite sure they would not touch his victuals. We now got upon an excessively bad road, so cut up that the horses could hardly drag the carriage through the deep ruts, and the soil being of the red, waxy kind, we found it almost as difficult to walk upon it. In the course of the day we met a great many families of planters emigrating to Alabama and Mississippi to take up cotton plantations, their slaves tramping through the waxy ground on foot, and the heavy waggons containing the black women and children slowly dragging on, and frequently breaking down. All that were able were obliged to walk, and being wet with fording the streams were shivering with cold. The negroes suffer very much in these expeditions conducted in the winter season, and upon this occasion must have been constantly wet, for I am sure we forded from forty to fifty streams this day, which, although insignificant in dry weather, were at this time very much swollen with rain. We passed at least 1000 negro slaves, all trudging on foot, and worn down with fatigue.

The Indian cabins, as we advanced, were somewhat different from those we observed on entering the territory, being merely circular spaces covered with bark, and apparently exposed to all the rains: on examining them, however, I found that a small trench was dug round them which prevented the superficial water getting in, and that the bark was lapped over so well that it kept all the rain out. But no language can describe the filth inside of them, and the disgusting appearance of their tenants, especially the old crones. The women seemed to be fond of being bled, for in one of the largest cabins a young man had been bleeding several of them with a rude lancet. Amongst the rest was an old creature turned sixty, the most thoroughly hideous, wrinkled, dark, and dirty hag I had ever seen amongst them: she had the features and hair of an Alecto, and was completely stark naked.

We made only twenty-five miles this day, and arrived after dark excessively fatigued at one Cook's, a cheerful, dissipated sort of fellow; whose wife, however, being a very respectable woman, gave us a tolerable clean supper and separate beds. In the morning I found that Mr. Cook was a collector of natural curiosities, the stuffed skins of three extraordinarily thick *Diamond rattlesnakes* being hung up in the porch of his little tavern, one of which was seven feet ten inches long, and thirteen inches and a quarter in circumference. He said that great numbers of these enormous snakes, which I believe have not yet been described, were found in the pine lands of this part of the Creek nation. There is also some limestone near his house, in which I observed imperfect specimens of Gryphaea vesiculosa. From hence we got into a very pretty sandy district, and found a tolerably good road on the sand ridges. Streams, whose banks were covered with laurels, live oaks, and other evergreens, were running pleasingly at the base of graceful pine hills, which overlaid a rotten limestone, and wild grass was growing every where in great profusion. This day we met an almost uninterrupted line of emigrants, with innumerable heavy and light waggons. Some of them had got stuck fast in the deep bottoms, and the men around them were pulling, hauling, whipping, and cursing and swearing to get them out; there were also some lighter carriages, indicating a better class of emigrants. Amongst the rest was an old-fashioned gig, with a lame horse guided by an aged grandmother, with several white and black children stuck in it around her. The whole scene would have reminded me of the emigrations in patriarchal times, but for the very decided style of the cursing and swearing. As we advanced they all inquired if the road was not better a-head; and our answer generally was, "Keep up your spirits and you'll get through." At one time of the day we certainly passed 1200 people, black and white, on foot. We found very few Indians in this part of the territory—a circumstance I was glad of, as the spectacle they furnished was always a distressing one; and occasionally some of the young men, who were rather drunk, had been very insolent to us.

About eight miles before we reached the Chatahoochie we met boulders of gneiss and quartz, always an indication, in this part of North America, of the limits of the subcretaceous and tertiary beds. In the afternoon we reached the Chatahoochie, it having taken us four days to travel a distance of ninety miles. This fine stream is crossed by an excellent bridge, and divides the state of Georgia from the Creek territory now forming part of Alabama. On the opposite bank is the pretty town of Columbus, in Georgia, where we stopped for the night at a noisy tavern, which seemed to be a general boarding-house for the town. My first care was to secure places for the mail-stage in the morning; the next, to hasten to the Falls of the Chatahoochie, about a mile from Columbus, where I had the pleasure of meeting the gneiss rocks again in place, and of seeing this fine river tumble over them just as it does at Fredericsburgh and Richmond, in Virginia: indeed, there is a strong scenic resemblance betwixt the falls of all the rivers on the east side of the chain which fronts the Atlantic. After gratifying my curiosity, I recrossed the bridge to the Indian side of the Chatahoochie, where I saw a great many huts, and some dwellings apparently belonging to white persons. Here I found the lowest stage of drunkenness and debauchery, prevailing to such an extent that the settlement had acquired the nickname of Sodom [Girard; today's Phenix City]: and on my return into Columbus the street was swarming with drunken Indians, and young prostitutes, both Indian and white, a sufficient indication of the manners of the place.

13

Harriet Martineau
April 1835

⚜

H ARRIET MARTINEAU (1802-1876), REARED AS A STRICT UNITAR-
IAN IN A MANUFACTURING FAMILY, EVENTUALLY TURNED TO MES-
MERISM AND ATHEISM. BUT SHE FIRST ROSE TO NATIONAL PROMINENCE IN
ENGLAND BY WRITING POPULAR STORIES ILLUSTRATING THE POLITICAL
ECONOMY OF MALTHUS, RICARDO AND MILL. THE PROLIFIC WRITER WAS
LIONIZED IN LITERARY, ECONOMIC AND POLITICAL CIRCLES. TO REST FROM
HER WORK, SHE EMBARKED ON A TWO-YEAR AMERICAN JOURNEY. HER
OUTSPOKEN OPPOSITION TO SLAVERY NOTWITHSTANDING, SHE WAS WELL
RECEIVED IN THE SOUTH. IN BOSTON, HOWEVER, SHE WAS HORRIFIED BY
THE VIOLENCE AGAINST THE ABOLITIONISTS, A GROUP SHE HAD PREVI-
OUSLY THOUGHT FANATICAL. SHE RETURNED TO ENGLAND AN ABOLITION-
IST HERSELF—AFTER HAVING BEEN IGNORED BY THE RESPECTABLE CLASSES
AND ENDURING THREATS OF VIOLENCE IN THE NORTH, AND HAVING TO
ABANDON HER TOUR DOWN THE OHIO. ENGLISH PUBLISHERS AVIDLY
SOUGHT HER THREE-VOLUME ACCOUNT OF THE AMERICAN TRAVELS WITH
ITS DISCUSSION OF AMERICAN SOCIETY AND POLITICS.

Harriet Martineau. *Society in America*. Vols. 2. New York:
Saunders and Otley, 1837. Volume I, pages 214-219.

The Chattahoochee, on whose banks Columbus stands, is unlike
any river I saw in the United States, unless it be some parts of the
Susquehanna. Its rapids, overhung by beech and pine woods, keep
up a perpetual melody, grateful alike to the ear of the white and

the red man. It is broad and full, whirling over and around the rocks with which it is studded, and under the frail wooden foot-bridge which spans a portion of its width, between the shore and a pile of rocks in the middle of the channel. On this foot-bridge I stood, and saw a fish caught in a net laid among the eddies. A dark fisherman stood on each little promontory; and a group was assembled about some canoes in a creek on the opposite Alabama shore, where the steepness of the hills seemed scarcely to allow a foothold between the rushing water and the ascent. The river is spanned by a long covered bridge, which we crossed the same night on our way into Alabama.

There are three principal streets in Columbus, with many smaller, branching out into the forest. Some pretty bits of greensward are left, here and there, with a church, or a detached house upon each—village-like. There are some good houses, five hotels, and a population of above 2,000,—as nearly as I could make out among the different accounts of the accession of inhabitants since the census. The stores looked credibly stocked; and a great many gentlemanly men were to be seen in the streets. It bears the appearance of being a thriving, spacious, handsome village, well worth stopping to see.

We left it, at seven in the evening, by the long bridge, at the other end of which we stopped for the driver to hold a parley, about a parcel, with a woman, who spoke almost altogether in oaths. A gentleman in the stage remarked, that we must have got quite to the end of the world. The roads were as bad as roads could be; and we rolled from side to side so incessantly, as to obviate all chance of sleeping. The passengers were very patient during the hours of darkness; but, after daylight, they seemed to think they had been long enough employed in shifting their weight to keep the coach on its four wheels. "I say, driver," cried one, "you won't upset us, now daylight is come?" "Driver," shouted another, "keep this side up." "Gentlemen," replied the driver, "I shall mind nothing you say till the ladies begin to complain." A reply equally politic and gallant.

At half-past five, we stopped to breakfast at a log dwelling, composed of two rooms, with an open passage between. We asked for water and towel. There was neither basin nor towel; but a shallow tin dish of water was served up in the open passage where all our fellow-travellers were standing. We asked leave to carry our dish into the right-hand room. The family were not all dressed. Into the left-hand room. A lady lodged there!

We travelled till sunset through the Creek Territory, the roads continuing to be extremely bad. The woods were superb in their spring beauty. The thickets were in full leaf; and the ground was gay with violets, may-apple, buck-eye, blue lupin, iris, and crow-poison. The last is like the white lily, growing close to the ground. Its root, boiled, mixed with corn, and thrown out into the fields, poisons crows. If eaten by cattle, it injures but does not destroy them. The sour-wood is a beautiful shrub. To-day it looked like a splendid white fuchsia, with tassels of black butterflies hanging from the extremities of the twigs. But the grandest flower of all, perhaps the most exquisite I ever beheld, is the honeysuckle of the southern woods [wild azalea]. It bears little resemblance to the ragged flower which has the same name elsewhere. It is a globe of blossoms, larger than my hand, growing firmly at the end of an upright stalk, with the richest and most harmonious colouring, the most delicate long anthers, and the flowers exquisitely grouped among the leaves. It is the queen of flowers. I generally contrived, in my journeys through the southern States, to have a bunch of honeysuckle in the stage before my eyes; and they seemed to be visible wherever I turned, springing from the roots of the forest trees, or dangling from their top-most boughs, or mixing in with the various greens of the thickets.

We saw to-day, the common sight of companies of slaves travelling westwards; and the very uncommon one of a party returning into South Carolina. When we overtook such a company proceeding westwards, and asked where they were going, the answer commonly given by the slaves was, "Into Yellibama."—Sometimes these poor creatures were encamped, under the care of the slave-trader, on the banks of a clear stream, to spend a day in washing their clothes. Sometimes they were loitering along the road; the old folks and infants mounted on the top of a wagon-load of luggage; the able-bodied, on foot, perhaps silent, perhaps laughing;

the prettier of the girls, perhaps with a flower in the hair, and a lover's arm around her shoulder. There were wide differences in the air and gait of these people. It is usual to call the most depressed of them brutish in appearance. In some sense they are so; but I never saw in any brute an expression of countenance so low, so lost, as in the most degraded class of negroes. There is some life and intelligence in the countenance of every animal; even in that of "the silly sheep," nothing so dead as the vacant unheeding look of the depressed slave is to be seen. To-day, there was a spectacle by the roadside which showed that this has nothing to do with negro nature; though no such proof is needed by those who have seen negroes in favourable circumstances, and know how pleasant an aspect those grotesque features may wear. To-day we passed, in the Creek Territory, an establishment of Indians who held slaves. Negroes are anxious to be sold to Indians, who give them moderate work, and accommodations as good as their own. Those seen to-day among the Indians, were sleek, intelligent, and cheerful-looking, like the most favoured house-slaves, or free servants of colour, where the prejudice is least strong.

We were on the look-out for Indians, all the way through this Creek Territory. Some on horseback gave us a grave glance as we passed. Some individuals were to be seen in the shadow of the forest, leaning against a tree or a fence. One lay asleep by the roadside, overcome with "whiskey too much," as they style intoxication. They are so intent on having their full bargain of whiskey, that they turn their bottle upside down, when it has been filled to the cork, to have the hollow at the bottom filled. The piazza at the post-office was full of solemn Indians. Miserable-looking squaws were about the dwellings, with their naked children, who were gobbling up their supper of hominy from a wooden bowl.

We left the Creek Territory just as the full moon rose, and hoped to reach Montgomery by two hours before midnight. We presently began to ascend a long hill; and the gentlemen passengers got out, according to custom, to walk up the rising ground. In two minutes, the driver stopped, and came to tell us ladies that he was sorry to trouble us to get out; but that an emigrant's wagon had blocked up the ford of a creek which we had to cross; and he feared we might be wetted if we remained in the stage while he took it through a deeper part. A gentleman was waiting, he said, to hand us over the log which was to be our bridge. This gentleman, I believe, was the emigrant himself. I made for what seemed to me the end of the log; but was deceived by the treacherous moonlight, which made wood, ground, and water, look all one colour. I plunged up to the waist into the creek; and, when I was out again, could hardly keep upon the log for laughing. There was time, before we overtook the rest of the party, to provide against my taking cold; and there remained only the ridiculous image of my deliberate walk into the water.

It must not be supposed a common circumstance that an emigrant's wagon was left in a creek. The "camping out" is usually done in a sheltered, dry spot in the woods, not far from some little stream, where the kettle may be filled, and where the dusty children may be washed. Sleepy as I might be, in our night journeys, I was ever awake to this picture, and never tired of contemplating it. A dun haze would first appear through the darkness; and then gleams of light across the road. Then the whole scene opened. If earlier than ten at night, the fire would be blazing, the pot boiling, the shadowy horses behind, at rest, the groups fixed in their attitudes to gaze at us, whether they were stretching their sailcloth on poles to windward, or drawing up the carts in line, or gathering sticks, or cooking. While watching us, they little thought what a picture they themselves made. If after midnight, the huge fire was flickering and smouldering; figures were seen crouching under the sailcloth, or a head or two was lifted up in the wagon. A solitary figure was seen in relief against the fire; the watch, standing to keep himself awake; or, if greeted by our driver, thrusting a pine slip into the fire, and approaching with his blazing torch to ask or to give information. In the morning, the places where such encampments have been cannot be mistaken. There is a clear, trodden space, strewed with chips and refuse food, with the bare poles which had supported the sailcloth, standing in the midst, and a scorched spot where the fire had been kindled. Others, besides emigrants, camp out in the woods. Farmers, on their way to a distant market, find it cheaper to bring food, and trust otherwise to the hospitality of dame Nature, than to put up at hotels. Between the one and the other, we were amply treated with the untiring spectacle.

We had bespoken accommodations for the night at the hotel at Montgomery, by a friend who had preceded us. On our arrival at past eleven o'clock, we found we were expected; but no one would have guessed it.

14

P. T. Barnum
February 1837

🔱

P HINEAS TAYLOR BARNUM (1810-1891) HAD ONLY JUST BEGUN HIS
CAREER AS A SHOWMAN WHEN HE CROSSED CREEK TERRITORY ON
THE WAY TO MONTGOMERY. LATER HE WOULD DISCOVER THE BASES OF
POPULAR TASTE, NOT ONLY IN AMERICA, BUT ALSO IN ENGLAND. MORE-
OVER, HE PLAYED A LEADING ROLE IN DEFINING THAT TASTE WITH THE
AMERICAN MUSEUM OF CURIOSITIES IN NEW YORK CITY; AS PROMOTER
OF TOM THUMB, JENNY LIND AND JUMBO; AND AS FOUNDER OF "THE
GREATEST SHOW ON EARTH" AND PARTNER IN THE BARNUM AND BAILEY
CIRCUS.

Phineas Taylor Barnum. *The Life of P. T. Barnum*. New York:
Redfield, 1855. Pages 193-196.

In passing from Columbus, Georgia, to Montgomery, Alabama,
we were obliged to travel eighty miles through a very thinly settled
and desolate portion of country know as the "Indian Nation." At
this time our government was gathering in the Indians, and lodg-
ing them in encampments at various posts under a strong guard,
preparatory for their migration to Arkansas. The chief portion of
the Indians came in voluntarily, and were willing to be removed to
their new home; but there was a good number of "hostiles" who
would not come in, but who infested the swamps near the road
leading from Columbus to Montgomery, and who almost daily
murdered passengers who had occasion to pass through the "Indian Nation." Many considered it hazardous to pass over the road

without a strong escort. The day previous to our starting, the mail stage had been stopped, the passengers all murdered, and the stage burned, the driver escaping almost by a miracle. It was with much trepidation that we determined upon incurring the risk. Our chief hope was, that owing to the large number composing our company, and the Indians being scattered in small bands, our appearance would be too formidable for them to risk an attack. We all armed ourselves with guns, pistols, bowie-knives, etc., and started on our journey.

None of us felt ashamed to acknowledge that we dreaded to incur the risk, except Vivalla. He was probably the greatest coward amongst us, but like most of that class when they feel pretty *safe*, he swaggered and strutted about with much apparent importance, laughing at us for our fears, and swearing that he was afraid of nothing, but if he met fifty Indians "he should give them one devil of a licking, and send dem back to de swamp in no time." The cowardly little braggadocio vexed us much, and we determined if we ever got through to put his courage to the test.

The first day we travelled thirty miles without seeing any Indians, and before night came to a halt at the house of a cotton planter, who kept us safe till morning. The next day we proceeded safely to Tuskeega, a small village where there was an encampment of fifteen hundred Indians, including squaws and children. The third day we arrived at Mount Megs, where there was another "Indian camp" containing twenty-five hundred of the red skins. We were now within fourteen miles of Montgomery, and felt out of all danger. But being determined to play a trick upon the courageous Vivalla, we informed him the next morning that we had to pass over the most dangerous portion of the road, as it was said to be infested with desperate hostile warriors. Vivalla, as usual, was all courage; saying, "he only hoped he should see some of de copper-colored rascals; how he would make dem run." When we had travelled about six miles, and had come to a dismal-looking, thickly wooded place, a large fox squirrel crossed the road, and ran into the adjoining woods. Vivalla proposed pursuing it. This was just what we wanted; so giving a hint to several who were in the secret, we halted, and they went with Vivalla in pursuit of the squirrel. In the mean time Pentland slipped on an old Indian dress with a fringed hunting shirt and moccasins, which we had secretly purchased at Mount Megs, and coloring his face with Spanish brown, which we had obtained for the purpose, and mounting his head with a cap of colored feathers, he shouldered a musket and followed the track of Vivalla and his party, looking as much like a real Indian as any we had seen the day previous in the camp. When he had got near them, he approached stealthily, and was not discovered till he leaped in their very midst, and uttered a tremendous "whoop."

Vivalla's companions, who were all in the joke, instantly fled in the direction of the wagons, and Vivalla himself, half frightened to death, exhibited great swiftness of foot in his endeavors to take the same route, but the artificial Indian betrayed extreme partiality and malignity in allowing all the others to escape, and devoting his whole attention to "heading" the Italian. The poor little fellow yelled like a wild man, when he saw the musket of the Indian pointed towards him, and found there was no possible means of escape, except by running in the direction opposite to where we were waiting. He ran like a deer, jumping over fallen trees and stumps with remarkable quickness, not daring to look behind him. Pentland, who was the most nimble on foot, allowed the Italian to keep about four rods ahead, while he followed, gun in hand, uttering a horrible Indian yell at every other step. The race continued nearly a mile, when the Signor, completely out of breath, perceiving his red-skin adversary was fast gaining on him, stopped, and throwing himself on his knees begged for life. The Indian, pretending not to understand English, levelled his gun at Vivalla's head, but the poor fellow writhed and screeched like a panther; and carrying on a pantomime, gave the Indian to understand that life was all he asked, and if that was spared every thing he possessed was at the service of his foe. The savage appeared to relent, and to understand the signs made by the Italian. He took his musket by the muzzle and rested the breech upon the ground, at the same time motioning to his trembling victim to "shell out."

Quick as thought, Vivalla turned his pockets inside out, and the Indian seized his purse containing eleven dollars. This was all

THE COWARD AND THE "BRAVE."

the money he had about him, the rest being deposited in a trunk in
one of our wagons. Gloves, handkerchiefs, knives, etc., were next
offered up to appease the wrath of the savage; but he looked upon
the offerings with disdain. Then motioning the Italian to rise from
his knees, the poor follow got up, and was led by his conqueror
like a lamb to the slaughter. The savage marched him to a large
and stately oak, where he proceeded, with the aid of a handkerchief, to tie his arms in the most scientific and Indian-like manner
around the trunk of the tree.

The red-skinned warrior then departed, leaving poor Vivalla
more dead than alive. Pentland hastened to join us, and doffing his
wampum dress and washing his face, we all proceeded in quest of
the Italian. We found the little fellow tied to the tree, nearly dead
with fright, but when he saw us his joy knew no bounds. We loos-
ened his hands, and he jumped and laughed, and chattered like a
monkey. His courage returned instantly, and he swore that after
his companions left him, the Indian was joined by half a dozen
others; that if he had kept his gun he should have shot one and beat
out the brains of the other six, but being unarmed, he was obliged
to surrender. We pretended to believe his story, and allowed him

to repeat and brag over his adventures for a week afterwards, at which time we told him the joke. Chagrin and mortification sat on every line of his countenance, but he soon rallied and swore that it was all "one great lie." Pentland offered him his eleven dollars, but he would not touch it, for he "swore like a trooper" that it could not be his, for seven Indians took his money from him. Many a hearty laugh did we have over the valor of the little Italian, but we were at last obliged to drop the subject altogether, for the mere allusion to it made him so angry and surly that we could not get a pleasant word out of him for a week afterwards. But from that time we never heard the Signor boast of his courage, or make any threats against a foe, real or imaginary.

We reached Montgomery, Ala., February 28th, 1837. . . .

15

James Buckingham
March 1839
ॐ

ENGLISH-BORN JAMES SILK BUCKINGHAM (1786-1855) BEGAN HIS TRAVELS AT TEN WHEN HE FIRST WENT TO SEA. HE WAS A PRISONER OF THE FRENCH FOR SEVERAL MONTHS DURING THE NAPOLEONIC WARS. AT THIRTY-TWO HE FOUNDED A NEWSPAPER IN CALCUTTA, BUT FIVE YEARS LATER WAS EXPELLED FROM INDIA BECAUSE OF HIS OUTSPOKEN CRITICISM OF THE EAST INDIA COMPANY'S GOVERNMENT OF INDIA. OTHER PERIODICALS FOLLOWED IN ENGLAND. IN 1832 HE WAS ELECTED MEMBER OF PARLIAMENT FOR SHEFFIELD; HE ADVOCATED SOCIAL REFORM, TEMPERANCE, AND ABOLITION OF FLOGGING IN THE ARMY AND NAVY. IN 1837 HE RETIRED FROM PARLIAMENT, AND, FOLLOWING A FOUR-YEAR TOUR OF THE UNITED STATES AND CANADA, SERVED AS PRESIDENT OF THE LONDON TEMPERANCE LEAGUE. IN ADDITION TO SOCIAL AND POLITICAL SUBJECTS, HE WROTE ON HIS TRAVELS IN THE MIDDLE EAST AND WESTERN EUROPE. HE RECORDED HIS NORTH AMERICAN TRAVELS IN NINE VOLUMES, INCLUDING TWO-VOLUMES ABOUT THE SLAVE STATES.

Buckingham, James Silk. *The Slave States of America.* Vols. 2. London: Fisher, Son, and Company, 1842. Volume I, pages 250-260.

In this coach we left Columbus at eight o'clock on the morning of Wednesday the 13th of March [1839]; and crossing the river Chathahooche a little below the falls, by the wooden bridge described, we entered on the state of Alabama, the river being the dividing line or boundary between the two.

The change of aspect in scenery and condition was very striking. The woods, into which we were entering, seemed more wild, the road being a mere pathway through and around standing trees, the tops of which touched our heads in many places; the land was poorer in quality, but being more undulated in surface, the swamps in the bottoms were more abundant; the brooks ran with greater impetuosity, and the bridges over them were more rude than any we had yet seen. Rough corduroy roads occurred for many hundred yards at a time, and loose planks laid across horizontal beams, supported on single pillars, but neither nailed nor fastened, served for bridges; while frequently the coach would have to go through water deep enough to come close up to the coach-door, and threaten us, by the slightest false step, with immersion. The stations, where we changed horses, were mere log-huts, used as stables: and all the way, for miles in succession, we saw neither a human being, a fence, a rood of cleared land, nor anything indeed that could indicate the presence of man, or the trace of civilization, so that we felt the solitude of the woods in all its fulness.

This description applies to all the tract of land for many miles beyond the river Chathahoochee; and it was said that whoever came as far as that towards Georgia, were more disposed to go on and fix their settlement in that State, than in Alabama, which seems to have a bad name even among those who reside in it. Beyond this belt, signs of settlement began gradually to appear, but even these were of the rudest kind. A blacksmith's shop, a few log-huts, and a "confectionary," with the ever-ready poison of strong drink, constituted a village; and for forty miles of our road we saw only one instance of a store where any other goods could be procured; this being a log-house recently devoted to the purpose of a general drapery and grocery warehouse.

It was five o'clock, or nine hours after our setting out from Columbus, when we reached the little village of Tuskeegea, forty-five miles from Columbus; and here we should have halted for the night, but that there were yet two good hours of daylight, and we were desirous of making the second day's journey as short as practicable. The inn, at which we changed horses, was one of the neatest and cleanest we had seen in the South; and though very humble in its appearance and furniture, there was such an air of neatness, cleanliness, and order about it, that it excited our warm commendation. The landlady, having her sympathies touched by our praise of her management and arrangement, entered voluntarily into conversation with us, and told us the outline of her history.

She said that her husband and herself had both been brought up without having been taught the proper value of money, so that they had not been long married before they had run through all they possessed. In this extremity they had only a choice between two evils, one of which was to go to Texas, where people who were unfortunate had land given to them, and could get on fast, by industry and care; the other was to purchase a small piece of land in some rising village nearer home, and, by a little harder labour and more rigid economy, get on quite as well, though not quite so fast, as in Texas. They preferred the last, and came here about three years ago; it was then that the first tree was cut down to form the village of Tuskeegea, where some Creek Indians of that name had just vacated a settlement, to go beyond the Mississippi. These Indians, she said, had been a terror to all the whites of the neighbourhood, and massacred many families in cold blood; and her statement was confirmed to us in many quarters. Among other instances of their ferocity and cruelty, we heard at Columbus, that some years ago a stage-coach had been attacked by them in the forest, and after securing the horses for their own use, the Indians broke up the coach, and burnt it in the middle of the road. They then made the passengers prisoners, and scalping them all, men, women, and children, they placed them in a small wigwam, to which they set fire, and burnt them all alive! In Florida, to the present hour, the Seminoles commit similar outrages on the whites wherever they can find them; and we heard from two ladies going to St. Augustine, that within the last two years, nearly every white family living within two or three miles of these towns, had been put to death by the Indians.

Since the settlement of this landlady and her husband, who was a general, at Tuskeegee, they had prospered exceedingly, were every year adding to their substance, and surrounding themselves with comforts and means of enjoyment. A good population had been attracted near them, comprising upwards of 300 persons; and there was now an excellent school, in which more than 100 youths of both sexes received the best education given in the country, from a male teacher from Mobile, and a female teacher from the celebrated seminary at Troy, in the State of New York. The teachers were said to be very competent, and received 1000 dollars, or about 200*l*. a year each; and music, drawing, and languages were taught, as well as the ordinary branches of an English education. No village of 300 persons in England could certainly produce the parallel of this, more especially a village only three years old.

Our next stage from hence was a distance of twelve miles, through the same description of scenery as that passed in the morning, but the soil was more clayey, and the road better, though all our drive was performed through a deluge of heavy rain, which was very acceptable to the country, as more than a month had passed since any rain had fallen.

At the end of this stage we reached a log-house, where we were to sleep for the night. The beds and interior accommodations were most uninviting; but we had no choice, so, lighting a large wood-fire, and preparing some tea, which our kind friends at Savannah had furnished us with, as none was to be had in houses of this description, we enjoyed it, and retired early. During the night, the rain poured down with great violence, and as the roof of the log-house was not water-proof, we had streams entering at different part of it, which made our position very uncomfortable. The partitions between the several small apartments into which the house was divided, were so thin, and the beds were placed so close to them, that the slightest noise or sound made in one room could be distinctly heard in the next; so that it was like sleeping with a dozen persons in the same apartment. The cries of some young children, the snoring of the negroes scattered about lying on the floor, the constant barking of several large dogs, saluting and answering each other in alternate volleys, and the incessant croakings of the frogs, with which every part of these woods abound, made it almost impossible to sleep. We therefore got out to trim the fire, and see the hour, several times during the night, and were extremely glad when the daylight broke on us, our first perception of this being through the chinks of the roof, as there was no window whatever in the room in which we slept.

In the morning a very rude breakfast was prepared; and happening to converse with the old woman who served us, on the state of the country, and asking whether the removal of the Indians was not considered a blessing by the settlers here, I remarked that she made no answer. We afterwards learnt, that the man by whom the house was kept was himself a half-blood Indian, and his rage was said to be so great when this question was repeated to him, that he was "perfectly mad," in the language of our informant, and declared his regret that he had missed the opportunity to shoot me for so saying. Such is the vindictive spirit that seems to flow through Indian veins, and which loses but little of its original nature, even by mingling with gentler blood than its own.

We left this log-house at half-past eight, in the same coach that brought us from Tuskeegee; and proceeded onward for Montgomery, reaching, after a few miles, a new village settlement called Cubahatchee. The soil now became richer on each side, and the woods were much more variegated, as, besides the ever-succeeding pine, there was a thick under-wood of various flowering shrubs and trees, including magnolias, yellow jessamines, the dogwood, and the grape-vine, with a very beautiful tree called the willow-oak. The brooks of water were also more frequent, though the bridges over them were still of the rudest kind; and across one, the only road for foot-passengers was along a series of high-legged benches or forms, ranged in line, or end to end, elevated a few inches only above the water's-edge, and never more than eight or nine inches wide.

A little beyond Cubahatchee we passed one of the most spacious and best-built houses that we had yet seen on the road, with portico and verandas, an excellent garden surrounding it, and the whole enclosed with a regular paling of uniform upright pointed rails, smooth and painted white: pride-of-india trees were abundant, and a peach-orchard near was in full blossom. In the centre of an adjoining field, was seen the family burial-ground, railed in with a paling like the garden, with this difference only, that while the body of the rails was white, the pointed terminations above the horizontal band were black, as well as the arch over the entrance-gateway; giving it thus the air of a place of mourning.

Immediately beyond this large mansion, the road was lined on each side with extensive fields of the richest soil, perfectly cleared of all timber, and even the stumps of the trees rooted up and re-moved. Some of these fields appeared to be from fifty to eighty acres each in extent; and we here saw the first instance of hedges and ditches around the enclosures. These lands had been devoted to corn in all previous years, but the present high price of cotton had tempted the greatest number of the planters here to cultivate this plant, and they were "all going into cotton mightily," as our informant expressed himself, this year, in the hope of making their fortunes by it in the next. Cotton pays the landholder a return of twenty per cent. for his capital, when it sells even at ten cents per pound; and it is now sixteen cents. In ploughing the land, on which the negroes were now engaged, each plough had one horse and one man only, the same person holding the plough and guiding the horse with a rein. For manure, small heaps of the cotton-seed were spread at regular distances, and then scattered over the surface. Many planters appropriate the whole of the seed of each crop to this purpose, and get new seed every year from South Carolina; but some reserve a sufficient quantity of the old seed for sowing the land for the new crop, and either use the surplus as manure, or sell it.

Excellent as the soil was here, and rich and productive as all the fields around us seemed to be, the roads were even worse than usual, the corduroy ridges of round logs extending sometimes for upwards of a mile in continuity, and so violently shaking the coach, that though it was nearly new, and built with great strength, it broke down with us in the middle of the road. We were therefore obliged to get out, and walk about half a mile to a farm-house during the rain, while it was repairing. This was done by the assistance of negroes sent from the farm, with poles of wood, and such rude tools as they could obtain for the purpose. A very little labour from each adjoining plantation would put these roads in excellent condition; but the reason assigned for this not being applied is, that every planter considers himself only a temporary occupant of the plantation on which he is settled; he thus goes on from year to year, racking it out, and making it yield as much cotton or corn as he can in each year, without considering the future, holding himself ready to sell at a day's notice to any one who will give him what he considers to be the increased value of the estate. With the proceeds of this he is ready to go farther west in quest of another lot of land, which he is ready to clear, plant, improve, and then sell as before. Under this system of perpetual movement, every planter is averse to lay out money or labour in improving the roads of his particular district, as it is extremely improbable that he will live long in the same spot, to enjoy the benefit of such improvements. Added to this, a railroad is now in progress from Columbus to Montgomery, and is expected to be finished in the course of a year, when the ordinary roads will be abandoned for all but merely local conveyances.

Our coach being set up again, we proceeded on our way, and soon passed a very spacious and elegant mansion, with large verandas all round, a beautiful and extensive garden, with vineries, arbours, and alcoves; and shortly after we halted at a small village called Mount Meigs, of still more recent origin than Tuskeegee, but, like it, flourishing and increasing rapidly. The fields in all this neighbourhood appeared larger, cleaner, better cultivated, and more productive, than any we had seen on our way; and the whole of the farming operations seemed on a better scale than usual; but the roads were still so bad, that before we had gone far we had a second break-down, and thought, for some time, we should have to walk the rest of the way to Montgomery; but by the aid of the negroes from a neighbouring plantation, we were once more set up, and enabled to proceed.

During the interval, and while the coach was under repair, we had an opportunity of seeing the great bulk of the labourers on the plantation. These were all negro slaves; and their appearance and condition were not at all superior to those we saw at Savannah; the few garments they had being almost wholly in rags, and their persons and apparel so filthy, that it might be doubted whether either the one or the other were ever washed from one end of the year to the other.

While we were halting here, patching up our broken vehicle, and lamenting our frequent delays, we were passed by the "Express Mail," established between New York and New Orleans. Letters, printed slips of news, and prices of goods, of sufficient importance to warrant the extra expense in their conveyance, are sent by this mode between the two cities. A relay of horses is posted all the way at intervals of four miles, for which it requires a stud of 500 horses, in motion or in constant readiness for mounting. Each boy rides only twenty-four miles, twelve onward and twelve back, changing his horses twelve times in that distance; and for this purpose, and to supply vacancies by sickness and accidents, about 200 boys are employed, who gallop the whole way, and make good fourteen miles an hour, including all stoppages. The expense of this conveyance is so much greater that its return, that it will probably be given up.

About three o'clock in the afternoon we reached Montgomery, having been seven hours performing a distance of thirty miles, with two break-downs on the way; and glad enough we were to terminate this long and tedious land-journey, in which, for a distance of more than 400 miles, we had scarcely seen anything but interminable forests on either side of our path, except in the small spaces occupied by the few towns and villages in the way, and the inconsiderable portions in which a few patches of corn or cotton cultivation bordered the mere skirts of the road.

At Montgomery we found excellent quarters in the best hotel we had seen since leaving New York, superior even, as it seemed to us at least, to the hotels of Charleston and Savannah; and, being desirous of proceeding onward without delay, we embarked in the steam-boat, "Commerce," to go down the Alabama river to Mobile, a distance of nearly 500 miles, which these fine vessels perform in about forty-eight hours, their rate of speed exceeding ten miles an hour all the way.

16

Epilogue

Charles Lyell
January 1846

Alexander Mackey
1847

🕱

A decade after most Creeks were removed and their former lands opened to white settlement, the conditions of the territory seem not to have changed much. Travelers' interest in the Federal Road declined, and ended after the railroad was connected to West Point, Georgia, in 1851.

SIR CHARLES LYELL (1797-1875) WAS A PROMINENT GEOLOGIST WHEN HE FIRST VISITED THE UNITED STATES IN 1841. HE BELIEVED THAT TRAVEL AND FIELD OBSERVATION WERE INDISPENSABLE FOR HIS PROFESSION, AND BEGAN THIS LIFE-LONG PURSUIT AT TWENTY YEARS OF AGE. HE WAS A MEMBER OF LONDON'S GEOLOGICAL AND THE LINNEAN SOCIETIES, AND A FELLOW OF THE ROYAL SOCIETY. HIS PUBLISHED WORKS AND LECTURES—HE ATTRACTED AUDIENCES AVERAGING THREE THOUSAND IN BOSTON—WERE WELL RECEIVED. HE TRAVELED FROM COLUMBUS TO MONTGOMERY IN LATE JANUARY, 1846, ON THE SECOND OF FOUR TRIPS TO THE UNITED STATES. HIS TWO ACCOUNTS OF THE UNITED STATES DISPLAY THE JUDGMENT OF A KEEN OBSERVER OF NATURE—AND MAN.

Charles Lyell. *A Second Visit to the United States of North America*. Vols. 2. London: John Murry, 1849. Volume II, pages 31-41.

Hitherto we had travelled from the north by railway or steam-ship, but from Macon, on our way south, we were compelled to resort to the stage-coach, and started first for Columbus. For the first time, we remarked that our friends, on parting, wished us a *safe* journey, instead of a pleasant one, as usual. [The remainder of the paragraph is omitted as it deals with Lyell's experiences east of Columbus.]

Our coach was built on a plan almost universal in America, and like those used in some parts of France, with three seats, the middle one provided with a broad leather strap, to lean back upon. The best places are given to the ladies, and a husband is seated next his wife. There are no outside passengers, except occasionally one sitting by the driver's side. We were often called upon, on a sudden, to throw our weight first on the right, and then on the left side, to balance the vehicle and prevent an upset, when one wheel was sinking into a deep rut. Sometimes all the gentlemen were ordered to get out in the dark, and walk in the wet and muddy road. The coachman would then whip on his steeds over a fallen tree or deep pool, causing tremendous jolts, so that my wife was thrown first against the roof, and then against the sides of the lightened vehicle, having almost reason to envy those who were merely splashing through the mud. To sleep was impossible, but at length, soon after daybreak, we found ourselves entering the suburbs of Columbus; and the first sight we saw there was a long line of negroes, men, women, and boys, well dressed and very merry, talking and laughing, who stopped to look at our coach. On inquiry, we were told that it was a gang of slaves, probably from Virginia, going to the market to be sold.

Columbus, like so many towns on the borders of the granitic and tertiary regions, is situated at the head of the navigation of a large river, and the rapids of the Chatahoochie are well seen from the bridge by which it is here spanned. The vertical rise and fall of this river, which divides Georgia from Alabama, amounts to no less than sixty or seventy feet in the course of the year; and the geologist should visit the country in November, when the season is healthy, and the river low, for then he may see exposed to view, not only the horizontal tertiary strata, but the subjacent cretaceous deposits, containing ammonites, baculites, and other characteristic fossils. These organic remains are met with some miles below the town, at a point called "Snake's Shoals;" and Dr. Boykin showed us a collection of the fossils, at his agreeable villa in the suburbs. In an excursion which I made with Mr. Pond to the Upotoy Creek, I ascertained that the cretaceous beds are overlaid everywhere by tertiary strata, containing fossil wood and marine shells.

The last detachment of Indians, a party of no less than 500, quitted Columbus only a week ago for Arkansas, a memorable event in the history of the settlement of this region, and part of an extensive and systematic scheme steadily pursued by the Government, of transferring the Aborigines from the Eastern States to the Far-West.

Here, as at Milledgeville, the clearing away of the woods, where these Creek Indians once pursued their game, has caused the soil, previously level and unbroken, to be cut into by torrents, so that deep gullies may everywhere be seen; and I am assured that a large proportion of the fish, formerly so abundant in the Chatahoochie, have been stifled by the mud.

The water-power at the rapids has been recently applied to some newly-erected cotton mills, and already an anti-free-trade party is beginning to be formed. The masters of these factories hope, by excluding coloured men—or, in other words, slaves—from all participation in the business, to render it a genteel employment for white operatives; a measure which places in a strong light the inconsistencies entailed upon a community by slavery and the antagonism of races, for there are numbers of coloured mechanics in all these Southern States very expert at trades requiring much more skill and knowledge than the functions of ordinary work-people in factories. Several New Englanders, indeed, who have come from the North to South Carolina and Georgia, complain to me that they cannot push on their children here, as carpenters, cabinet-makers, blacksmiths, and in other such crafts, because the planters bring up the most intelligent of their slaves to these occupations. The landlord of an inn confessed to me, that, being a carrier, he felt himself obliged to have various kinds of work done by coloured artisans, because they were the slaves of planters who employed him in his own line. "They interfere," said he, "with the fair competition of white mechanics, by whom I could have got the work better done."

These Northern settlers are compelled to preserve a discreet silence about such grievances when in the society of Southern slave-owners, but are open and eloquent in descanting upon them to a stranger. They are struck with the difficulty experienced in raising money here, by small shares, for the building of mills. "Why," say they, "should all our cotton make so long a journey to the North, to be manufactured there, and come back to us at so high a price? It is because all spare cash is sunk here in purchasing negroes. In order to get a week's work done for you, you must buy a negro out and out for life."

From Columbus we travelled fifty-five miles west to Chehaw, to join a railway, which was to carry us on to Montgomery. The stage was drawn by six horses, but as it was daylight we were not much shaken. We passed through an undulating country, some-times on the tertiary sands covered with pines, sometimes in swamps enlivened by the green palmetto and tall magnolia, and occasionally crossing into the borders of the granitic region, where there appeared immediately a mixture of oak, hiccory, and pine. There was no grass growing under the pine trees, and the surface of the ground was everywhere strewed with yellow leaves, and the fallen needles of the fir trees. The sound of the wind in the boughs of the long-leaved pines always reminded me of the waves breaking on a distant sea-shore, and it was agreeable to hear it swelling gradually, and then dying away, as the breeze rose and fell. Observing at Chehaw a great many stumps of these firs in a new clearing, I was curious to know how many years it would take to restore such a forest if once destroyed. The first stump I examined measured 2 feet 5 inches in diameter at the height of 3 feet from the ground, and I counted in it 120 rings of annual growth; a second measured less by 2 inches in diameter, yet was 260 years old; a third, at the height of 2 feet above the ground, although 180 years old, was only 2 feet in diameter; a fourth, the oldest I could find, measured, at the height of 3 feet above its base, 4 feet, and presented 320 rings of annual growth; and I could have counted a few more had the tree been cut down even with the soil. The height of these trees varied from 70 to 120 feet. From the time taken to acquire the above dimensions, we may confidently infer that no such trees will be seen by posterity, after the clearing of the country, except where they may happen to be protected for ornamental purposes. I once asked a surveyor in Scotland why, in planting woods with a view to profit, the oak was generally neglected, although I had found many trunks of very large size buried in peat-mosses. He asked if I had ever counted the rings of growth in the buried trees, to ascertain their age, and I told him I had often reckoned up 300, and once upwards of 800 rings; to which he replied, "then plant your shillings in the funds, and you will see how much faster they would grow."

Before reaching Chehaw, we stopped to dine at a small log-house in the woods, and had prepared our minds, from outward appearances, to put up with bad fare; but, on entering, we saw on the table a wild turkey roasted, venison steaks, and a partridge-pie, all the product of the neighbouring forest, besides a large jug of delicious milk, a luxury not commonly met with so far south.

The railway cars between Chehaw and Montgomery consisted, like those in the North, of a long apartment, with cross benches and a middle passage. There were many travellers, and among them one rustic, evidently in liquor, who put both his feet on one of the cushioned benches, and began to sing. The conductor told him to put his feet down, and afterwards, on his repeating the offence, lifted them off. On his doing it a third time, the train was ordered to stop, and the man was told, in a peremptory tone, to get out immediately. He was a strong-built labourer, and would have been much more than a match for the conductor, had he resisted; but he instantly complied, knowing, doubtless, that the officer's authority would be backed by the other passengers, if they were appealed to. We left him seated on the ground, many miles from any habitation, and with no prospect of another train passing for many a long hour. As we go southwards, we see more cases of intoxication, and hear more swearing.

At one of the stations we saw a runaway slave, who had been caught and handcuffed; the first I had fallen in with in irons in the course of the present journey. On seeing him, a New Englander, who had been with us in the stage before we reached Chehaw, began to hold forth on the miserable condition of the negroes in Alabama, Louisiana, Mississippi, and some other States which I had not yet visited. For a time I took for granted all he said of the sufferings of the coloured race in those regions, the cruelty of the overseers, their opposition to the improvement and education of the blacks, and especially to their conversion to Christianity. I began to shudder at what I was doomed to witness in the course of my further journeyings in the South and West. He was very intelligent, and so well informed on politics and political economy, that at first I thought myself fortunate in meeting with a man so competent to give me an unprejudiced opinion on matters of which he had been an eye-witness. At length, however, suspecting a disposition to exaggerate, and a party-feeling on the subject, I gradually led him to speak of districts with which I was already familiar, especially South Carolina and Georgia. I immediately discovered that there also he had everywhere seen the same horrors and misery. He went so far as to declare that the piny woods all around us were full of hundreds of runaways, who subsisted on venison and wild hogs; assured me that I had been deceived if I imagined that the coloured men in the upper country, where they have mingled more with the whites, were more progressive; nor was it true that the Baptists and Methodists had been successful in making proselytes. Few planters, he affirmed, had any liking for their negroes; and, lastly, that a war with England about Oregon, unprincipled as would be the measure on the part of the democratic faction, would have at least its bright side, for it might put an end to slavery. "How in the world," asked I, "could it effect this object?" "England," he replied, "would declare all the slaves in the

South free, and thus cripple her enemy by promoting a servile war. The negroes would rise, and although, no doubt, there would be a great loss of life and property, the South would nevertheless be a gainer by ridding herself of this most vicious and impoverishing institution." This man had talked to me so rationally on a variety of topics so long as he was restrained by the company of Southern fellow-passengers from entering on the exciting question of slavery, that I now became extremely curious to know what business had brought him to the South, and made him a traveller there for several years. I was told by the conductor that he was "a wrecker;" and I learnt, in explanation of the term, that he was a commercial agent, and partner of a northern house which had great connexions in the South. To him had been assigned the unenviable task, in those times of bankruptcy and repudiation which followed the financial crisis of 1839-40, of seeking out and recovering bad debts, or of seeing what could be saved out of the wreck of insolvent firms or the estates of bankrupt planters. He had come, therefore, into contact with many adventurers who had been over-trading, and speculators who had grown unscrupulous, when tried by pecuniary difficulties. Every year, on revisiting the Free States, he had contrasted their progress with the condition of the South, which by comparison seemed absolutely stationary. His thoughts had been perpetually directed to the economical and moral evils of slavery, especially its injuriousness to the fortunes and characters of that class of the white aristocracy with which he had most to do. In short, he had seen what was bad in the system through the magnifying and distorting medium of his own pecuniary losses, and had imbibed a strong anti-negro feeling, which he endeavoured to conceal from himself, under the cloak of a love of freedom and progress. While he was inveighing against the cruelty of slavery, he had evidently discovered no remedy for the mischief but one, the hope of which he confessedly cherished, for he was ready to precipitate measures which would cause the Africans to suffer that fate which the aboriginal Indians have experienced throughout the Union.

When I inquired if, in reality, there were hundreds of runaway slaves in the woods, every one laughed at the idea. As a general rule, they said, the negroes are well fed, and, when they are so, will very rarely attempt to escape unless they have committed some crime: even when some punishment is hanging over them, they are more afraid of hunger than of a whipping.

Although we had now penetrated into regions where the schoolmaster has not been much abroad, we observed that the railway cars are everywhere attended by news-boys, who, in some places, are carried on a whole stage, walking up and down "the middle aisle" of the long car. Usually, however, at each station, they, and others who sell apples and biscuits, may be seen calculating the exact speed at which it is safe to jump off, and taking, with the utmost coolness, a few cents in change a moment before they know that the rate acquired by the train will be dangerous. I never witnessed an accident, but as the locomotive usually runs only fifteen miles an hour, and is some time before it reaches half that pace, the urchins are not hurried as they would be in England. One of them was calling out, in the midst of the pine-barren between Columbus and Chehaw, "A novel, by Paul le Koch, the Bulwer of France, for 25 cents—all the go!—more popular than the Wandering Jew," &c. Newspapers for a penny or two-pence are bought freely by the passengers; and, having purchased them at random wherever we went in the Northern, Middle, Southern, and Western States, I came to the conclusion that the press of the United States is quite as respectable as our own. In the present crisis the greater number of prints condemn the war party, expose their motives, and do justice to the equitable offers of the English ministry in regard to Oregon. A large portion of almost every paper is devoted to literary extracts, to novels, tales, travels, and often more serious works. Some of them are especially devoted to particular religious sects, and nearly all of this class are against war. There are also some "temperance," and, in the North, "anti-slavery" papers.

We at length arrived at Montgomery, on the river Alabama, where I staid a few days to examine the geology of the neighbourhood.

THE YOUNG SCOT ALEXANDER MACKAY (1808-1852) WORKED AS A JOURNALIST IN CANADA. HE TRAVELED EXTENSIVELY IN CANADA AND THE UNITED STATES BEFORE TAKING A POSITION WITH A LONDON NEWSPAPER. HE RETURNED TO THE UNITED STATES IN 1846 TO REPORT ON THE OREGON COUNTRY QUESTION. SUBSEQUENTLY HE BECAME A LAWYER AND INVESTIGATED COTTON GROWING IN INDIA FOR ENGLISH COMMERCIAL INTERESTS. FOR MANY YEARS HIS THREE-VOLUME ACCOUNT OF THE UNITED STATES WAS THE MOST THOROUGH WORK ON THE COUNTRY.

Alexander Mackay. *The Western World: or, Travels in the United States in 1846-47*. Volumes 2. Philadelphia: Lea and Blanchard, 1849. Volume II, pages 64-65.

I left Columbus, after a brief stay, for Montgomery. Between these two places, the country is wild but not uninteresting. On crossing the Chatahouchee into Alabama, it seemed as if I had passed from an old country into a new. And such, indeed, was the case, the western part of Georgia having been much earlier settled and much longer cultivated than the more easterly belt of the conterminous State. For some time after entering Alabama my road led through a portion of the territory which had once been the domain of the Cherokees and the Creeks, but of which they had been divested by means which the American casuist may fancy himself able to justify. Well aware that the better regions of Alabama were before me, I was not disappointed with the sample of it presented along the road between the frontier and Montgomery. The land was not of the most fertile description, neither could it be called poor. For two-thirds of the way, it was only at long intervals that anything like clearances were to be seen, and it was only in the neighbourhood of Montgomery that I came to what might be termed regular plantations, with anything like decent or comfortable habitations upon them. On these I could see the slaves at work, on either side of the road; their condition betokening, at a glance, the character of their owner, some being well clad, apparently well fed, and hilarious in their dispositions; and others in rags, with their physical frames but poorly supported, and their spirits seemingly much depressed. For the whole way the road was excessively bad, and had it not been for a couple of days' dry weather, I do not know how we could have overcome them.

As a town, Montgomery is not calculated to leave so pleasing an impression upon the mind of the stranger as either Macon or Columbus. I stayed in it but an hour or two, during which I ascertained that it could offer very excellent accommodation to the traveller. After arriving I took the first steamer for Mobile, and found myself, in a little more than two hours after quitting the detestable stage-coach, steaming at the rate of eleven miles an hour down the winding channel of the Alabama.

Index

153